THOSE WIDE OPEN SPACES

HANK WILLIAMS

HOLE IN THE WALL PRESS

Sanford • Florida

InSync Communications LLC and Hole in the Wall Press
2445 River Tree Circle
Sanford, FL 32771
http://www.insynchronicity.com

ISBN: 1-929902-03-4
Library of Congress Catalog Number:
Williams, Hank, 1934
Those Wide Open Spaces

First Hole in the Wall Press Edition
10 9 8 7 6 5 4 3 2

Hole in the Wall Press books are available at special discounts when purchased in bulk for use in seminars, as premiums or in sales promotions. Special editions or book excerpts can also be created to specification. For details, contact InSync Communications LLC at the address above.

Special thanks for photo contributions and moral support:
Laura Bates, Founder, Hopalong Cassidy Fan Club, Mr. & Mrs. William Boyd on Dedication Page; Grace Bradley Boyd; Eddy Waller, photo on page 20; NTA, Inc., photo on page 68; John W. Leonard for help throughout Chapter 7; Bob Brown for photographs through Chapter 9; Donald R. Key, Empire Publishing; Roger M. Crowley, The Old West Shop; Howard and Martha Cherry; and Dave Holland

Cover Design by Jonathan Pennell

Printed in the United States of America

DEDICATION

THIS BOOK IS DEDICATED to my childhood hero, Hoppy, and one of the most beautiful, sweet and gracious ladies in the world — his widow, Grace Bradley Boyd — Mrs. Hopalong Cassidy. Together, they were the perfect couple.

Thank you grace for the conversation we had in Cambridge, Ohio about our favorite subject — "Hoppy". The reason I attended the "1999 Hopalong Cassidy Festival" was to meet you. Mr. Jerry Rosenthal ask me if I was coming to the festival and I told him I would come under one condition: that I would get to meet you and have my picture taken with you!

Love Ya Grace,

Hank Williams

CONTENTS

ABOUT THE AUTHOR

HANK WILLIAMS WAS BORN IN JANUARY 1934 in a small rural community of farmers in Cumberland Furnace, Tennessee. Throughout his life he served two tours in the U.S. Army, played semi-pro baseball, co-wrote a couple of songs, and produced a session at Columbia studios in Nashville. It was there that he saw the framed gold plated record of Gene Autry's *Silver Haired Daddy of Mine* which was the first Gold record in the industry.

Hank owned and operated a small film company. He wrote and produced advertising films that were shown on theatre screens, drive-in and indoor cinemas. Some of the films were used on television. At one time he booked and promoted country music shows for some of Nashville's stars — several from the TV's *Hee Haw*.

He coached junior-college baseball for five years and American Legion baseball during the summer months before moving to Florida. As the mayor of the city where

Hank lived once reminded him, he was always working as a baseball coach and manager. Hank Williams is a person who cares for the youth of our communities and takes both his time and money to prove it!

Known by his friends as an entrepreneur with a keen insight into the future, he is never without a new project to keep busy. At the age of 66 he loves golf and collecting Hopalong Cassidy B-Western memorabilia. His office looks like a small Hopalong Cassidy museum. This book is his first literary production. Currently Hank lives in Florida with his wife Ann, and their beloved Welsh corgi, Chelsea — who loves to watch Hoppy movies. When she hears Hoppy's contagious laugh, she races to the front door thinking the love of her life is coming to see her. Jimmy Blanks, a pro golfer on the National Senior Tour, the gentleman that got Hank interested in the game of golf, has a contagious laugh just like Hoppy's and Chelsea can't tell them apart.

ACKNOWLEDGMENTS

THE PHENOMENAL POPULARITY OF THOSE
Saturday afternoon movie cowboys didn't just happen.
There had to be something special about those men
whose presence touched so many of us in such a mean-
ingful way for all those many years.

My love and romance for those Saturday afternoon
heroes, and my research for this book, started over sixty
years ago — one Saturday afternoon at the State Theater
in Elizabethtown, Kentucky. I really loved William
Boyd… playing the role of Hopalong Cassidy…letting me
ride along beside him and Topper on that broom stick
pony of mine…on those wonderful Saturday afternoons.
I want to send a special Thank You to Grace Bradley Boyd
— Hoppy's lovely, gracious widow. Thanks a million,
Pretty Lady!

To Bob Brown, thanks for all the little stories and great
pictures, and thank you again for the great job you did on
making my Hoppy gun belt and holster. To John W.

Leonard, thanks for your help on Wild Bill Elliott. Thanks to Donald R. Key of Empire Publishing and Roger M. Crowley of *The Old West Shop* and Howard and Martha Cherry for some great pictures. And thanks so much, Dave Holland for the great pictures you shot, of Lone Pine for me. This book is made better as a result of your photographs—a great cover with a beautiful scene of those Alabama rocks, where Hoppy, Roy and Gene rode in the movies on those wonderful Saturday afternoons.

Yes, and a great big thank you to all the authors who wrote and edited so many good books on these Saturday matinee heroes. As time goes by, and so many of our matinee heroes are leaving us, the books these people are creating and have written become even more important to us and to the history of our great Saturday afternoon Westerns. It is these writers and their publishers who will keep the legacy alive for those silver screen cowboys have left us. I hope they will keep on writing about those happy days of our youth and the cowboy hero that had such an influence on our lives.

Special thanks goes to those great filmmakers who made possible all the cowboy movies of the B-Western period. Thanks to Grace Bradley Boyd for seeing that the Hopalong Cassidy films — along with the work of some other great Republic cowboy stars — were preserved and made available to us on video through Hopalong Cassidy Enterprises in Tarzana, CA.

Now that most of our Saturday afternoon cowboy heroes are no longer with us, let us not turn our backs on them as Hollywood did. It is you writers, publishers and collectors, as well as the hard-working people who put on those great festivals that will keep the legends alive. Since starting on this book four of our great singing cowboys, Roy, Gene, Eddie Dean, and Rex Allen, as well as the great Clayton Moore, have gone on to that great range in the sky.

I still find myself day dreaming about those fabulous days of youth — wishing again for those days of our Saturday afternoon Western heroes. There are men today, like myself, who were guided down the right trail because of those great heroes. Maybe, just maybe, this book will bring back some great memories that you can relive again. I must say, "I was never disappointed in my cowboy heroes." I wonder how many of the youth of America will be able to say these words about their heroes 60 years from now!

PUBLISHER'S COMMENT

CAN ANY OF YOU REMEMBER sitting in a tree, waiting for the imaginary bad guys to ride by so you could ambush them? Did you ever sit by a stream and believe you and your trusting steed were catching a breather between battles with bank robbers or Indians? How many garage roofs or tree branches did you jump from in an attempt to stop runaway stagecoaches? And was I the only young boy to actually hide his true persona in school, so that the teachers didn't notice that I was really a cowboy hero disguised as an elementary school boy?

I can remember, clear as anything, proudly wearing my Hopalong Cassidy ring to school. It was silver — well, it was silver in color. Hoppy's smiling face, under his big hat, completely covered the breadth of the ring finger on my right hand. I was very proud. Little did I know how that ring would one day play a decisive role in my personal growth and well-being.

One Spring day in 1952, after a long day in fifth grade, as I left the school building—one of those great stone structures with an actual belfry that dated from the late 1800's —I noticed, as much as I didn't want to, two of the schools toughest bullies. They were obviously waiting for some poor sucker to wander in their direction, and it seemed that I was the lucky sucker. It didn't take much to spark them into action: maybe it was the way one dressed, the lunch box you carried, or perhaps some other critically-important aspect of your life that they disliked. But, whatever it was, they did spring into action. The two —Larry who was twice my size and Paul who, while being no bigger than me, was obviously possessed by his own devils — began to circle me. I knew that this was my day to meet the playground face first.

Little did I know that I had taken on super-human powers that day. When I dressed that morning, besides my routine clothing, I had donned my Hopalong Cassidy ring. The power that ring bestowed on me was an unknown quantity — that is until one of those bullies hit me. The sudden impact of his fist hitting me must have shaken something loose, because before I was aware of it, I was raining punches into these guys the way only a Saturday-afternoon cowboy hero could have thrown punches. Before the fight had started, it was over. Paul, the feisty one, was wearing a bloody cut under his left eye. The ring had delivered the cut on his face. Noticing the blood on his pal's face, Larry took off running; Paul was only steps behind him.

I turned in surprise, looked at my right hand, and noticed that Hoppy was still smiling — perhaps more broadly than before the fight had started. My heart was in my throat as I spun around to watch them running off the school grounds, passed a car that was just pulling up to the curb. In that car was my mother. She waved to me and received the biggest possible wave in return. Little did she know of the exploits I had just experienced — that is, Hopalong Cassidy and me. It was only years later that I would share the details of that fight with her; she just wouldn't have understood at the time. But I did share it with my brother that night after the lights were turned out — in the privacy of our bedroom. What a story it was…and what a story it would become as the years went by.

That fight and many other events of my early boyhood were peppered with stimuli that came from Western heroes. I recall so many of them. There was the time that

I was so thrilled to have my cousins come to visit. I hadn't seen them since their father (a lifer in the Army) had taken the entire family to post-war Japan on a tour of duty in the later 1940's. Even though they were girls, there was a role for them in our cowboy games. I was Roy Rogers; my cousin Donna was Hopalong Cassidy; my other cousin Doreen was Lash LaRue. The unfortunate part of being the youngest in the group is that you often get stuck (for reasons that no one can explain) with a role you don't want to play. That is what happened to my brother, Gary. He got stuck playing the role of Dale Evans. Why? To this day, no one can explain why. I just recall his whining about it.

I carried a Hopalong Cassidy lunch box to school in fifth grade. My entire family listened to **Gunsmoke** on the radio every Sunday night while we ate dinner. I had cowboy board games. I wore cowboy clothing — a complete Roy Rogers' outfit (which I saw at a flea market for $600 in 1998) and a complete Hoppy outfit — both complete with boots, guns and holsters, and hats. I collected trading cards with pictures of Western heroes all through the elementary years. I read every cowboy comic book that I could get my hands on in the 1950's; and when I went into the Air Force, one of the most painful times of my life came when I went home on leave to find that my mother had "cleaned" my room for the first time in nearly a decade. That's right; she cleaned up everything—including my comic book and trading card collections. What today would be worth a small ransom was doomed to the local dump in a single moment of motherliness.

To this day I can still recall scenes from old Westerns—like still shots in my mind. Certain cowboys stayed in my brain, their movements emblazoned forever. Smaller than most heroes, I recall how Bob Steele stood up to his enemies like a giant. There was always a question as to exactly what would it take to have a "good guy" loose his hat during a fight? Just how did those guys jump so exactly as to place themselves into the saddle without hurting themselves—I just knew from personal experience that it didn't work that way when you tried to jump onto your Schwinn in the same manner. How many times could a chase take the hero and the bad guys past those same rocks? And what was the story on those stagecoaches with the little cutout area under the seats, where it appeared that someone was hiding and actually controlling those horses during the runaway scenes?

In the small town where I grew up along the Schuylkill River in Pennsylvania, we weren't fortunate enough to have our own movie theater. So on those Saturdays when allowed to venture across the river to the neighboring town (the rival football town), we'd pay our money to sit inside the "newly refrigerated" Penn Theater and watch everything from serials to features. These were the days of "coming attractions," cartoons (numerous cartoons), an episode of a serial, a feature (in color, if you were lucky), and even those boring news-of-the-day segments. We'd come out of those flicks with our heads spinning — and it wasn't just from the over exposure to the refrigerated air. Sure, we were beginning to meet girls at the movie theater in those years, but for most of us, the real thrill still came from the heroes on the screen. I don't think I shook the influence of the cowboys until I was well into my teens — and unfortunately, by those days the cowboys were disappearing from the silver screen all together.

It seems that my puberty and the demise of the movie cowboy were events that paralleled each other. As I got older, so did the cowboy stars. My needing a first shave and Hollywood's need to shut down production on the old B-Western occurred about the same time. I've always told my sons that they should put off their first shave as long as possible. I also think Hollywood might have prolonged youth for many of us — and themselves — by putting off the demise of the matinee cowboy. In my later years in high school, I recall a movie production company coming into my hometown to shoot a film. No, it wasn't a western — not in Pennsylvania. It was Steve McQueen's first motion picture. And even though old Steve would become popular for his **Wanted Dead or Alive** TV series, this film was a sci-fi feature: **The Blob**. Perhaps our country could have been better off if only it could have retained its youth for a few more years. It seems that the end of the cowboy movie era was also the beginning of this country's plunge into the "growing-up-too-quick" era.

This book has been fun to produce and a real step back into my youth. Thanks to Hank Williams for the opportunity to work with him on this testament to youthful dreams and unforgotten imagination.

Dennis McClellan
Publisher

FOREWORD

THE GREAT AMERICAN HERO

THE GREATEST AMERICAN HERO is the cowboy. It doesn't matter if he's the good guy in the white hat, a bad guy in black or an in-between mythic figure. The cowboy is all American and is what the rest of the world associates with America. It's that fascination that spawned the Italian and Spanish spaghetti westerns. The cowboys and the West comprise a folklore that is uniquely American — as much a part of American history and culture as the signing of the Declaration of Independence or baseball, hot dogs, and apple pie.

The popularity of the B-Western was an extension of the cowboy myth in American life. The wild-western tale with its miracle rider — sometimes a singing cowboy-hero — is the Great American Myth — The National Fairy Tale. That myth was about a world that never was but ought to have been — it is not now, but should be.

THOSE WIDE OPEN SPACES

The cowboy-hero received admiration and loyalty of amazing proportions. Millions of kids throughout the United States fantasized about becoming one of these Saturday afternoon heroes. Roy Rogers, Gene Autry, and Hopalong Cassidy took us back to the days of quick-draw, frontier justice, and two-gun-toting singing cowboys. Whether at the real O.K. Corral or on the silver screen at the local movie house, the tales, characters and mythical spirit remained the same: colorful, vibrant and exciting. The legends, characters, history, the tall tales — the B-Western movie was a celebration of an American tradition!

The western movie has been pronounced dead—replaced by what? Sex and violence operas! Who, may I ask, would have ever imagined it! Hell, Westerns are not dead! The Hollywood moviemakers simply cannot produce anyone capable of making a decent western—except maybe once in a Clint Eastwood while. Those great Saturday matinees are not likely to return, but where are the filmmakers that will fill the boots left vacant by John Ford, Howard Hawks and George Marshall? Those were creative Stylists who felt at home in and understood about the west.

Today, there are only film school graduates, saying less in two hours than a single scene by John Ford. The type of actors suited for westerns seem to be missing. Are you and I to be convinced that stage actor Kevin Kline is a handy man with gun and horse in *Silverado*. I don't think so! There is a new breed of hero today!

Did you have a cowboy hero when you were growing up? I bet you did! Was it Roy Rogers, Gene Autry, Hopalong Cassidy, Wild Bill Elliott, Allan "Rocky" Lane, Buck Jones, Tom Mix, Ken Maynard, The Durango Kid, The Cisco Kid, The Lone Ranger, or even maybe "Gabby" Hayes or Smiley Burnette. The question arises: **Who is the most popular cowboy of all time?**

Hollywood movie studios made a hell of a lot of money from the western attachment it turned its back on! But before those backs were turned, who were the top five western cowboys? Well, from 1936 to 1954 the Motion Picture Herald polled theatre exhibitors to determine an annual top western box office star. The all time toppers: No surprise #1 was Roy Rogers, "King of the Cowboys." Gene Autry the worlds most popular singing cowboy was #2, and coming in #3 was William Boyd, aka Hopalong Cassidy. Wild Bill Elliott — in my opinion, the most colorful cowboy of them all came in at #4. Charles "The Durango Kid" Starrett was # 5 on the list.

Other Than Gabby Hayes and Smiley Burnette who were tops, the other most popular sidekicks of all time, were Russell "Lucky" Hayden, Andy Devine and Fuzzy Knight.

These were my picks also for the top five spots, but I went a little farther and picked my "Great Eight" — the five already listed plus: Johnny Mack Brown who starred in 111 B-Westerns (who's numbers were only topped by Charles Starrett at Columbia Studios). Next is Tex Ritter, one of the better singing cowboys, who offered proof of his talent when, in January 1945 Tex had the top three songs on the famous *Billboard* chart:

1. *I'm Wastin' My Tears On You*
2. *There's a New Moon Over My Shoulder*
3. *Jealous Heart*

Tex Ritter, in 1937 finished 6th on the "Top Ten Money Making Western Stars" list and would make the list seven times in his career.

My other member of the "Great Eight" is Allen "Rocky" Lane. You got your money's worth when you went to see an Allen "Rocky" Lane movie. He played the cowboy role as good, if not better than any of the Saturday-afternoon western heroes.

THE GREAT EIGHT

1. Roy Rogers
2. Gene Autry
3. William Boyd (Hoppy)
4. Bill Elliott (Red Ryder)
5. Charles Starrett (Durango Kid)
6. Johnny Mack Brown
7. Allen "Rocky" Lane
8. Tex Ritter

I have always been intrigued with and fascinated by these silver-screen cowboy heroes and their colorful sidekicks, the heavies, as well as the character actors. And, of course, any great cowboy star had to have a beautiful horse or he was no hero of mine. "The Great Eight" — Oh my! Did they ever have some of the greatest horses that ever rode across a movie screen.

There was Roy and Trigger, Gene and Champion, Hoppy and Topper, Bill Elliott and Thunder, The Durango Kid and Raider, Johnny Mack Brown and Rebel, Allen "Rocky" Lane and Black Jack, and then there was Tex Ritter and his beautiful White Flash. These durable four-legged animals were exceptionally talented and could perform in their own way before the cameras — and on cue! Some of these great animals had their own comic books. Many of the sagebrush heroes had comic books and their horses had comic books selling along side their masters on the newsstands.

If you're like me, you remember the names of these exciting cowboys of yesteryear's silver screens. Even if you are a youngster in your 30's or 40's these names are familiar to you. Names like Rogers, Autry, Cassidy, Elliott, Lane, Starrett, Brown, and Ritter.

You are invited to sit back, relax and once again ride through those wide open spaces that we loved so well with these eight great cowboy heroes of those by-gone days. Not only these eight but you can visit for a while with other silver screen heroes, twenty six in all, and I'm sure you will find your favorite cowboy hero somewhere among these pages. In addition, there are ten "Silver Screen Saddle Queens" that you can see and visit. You will find the names of one hundred famous horses. See if you know and remember their riders.

WIDE OPEN SPACES

*Take me back to those wide open spaces
when a friend is a friend and where a pal is a pal
right or wrong, right or wrong.
I can hear the banjos ringing,
by the evening's campfire's gleam.
I can hear the cowhands singing,
out where the cowboys dream.
Oh, what I'd give just to live in God's country
with the sage and the clover, let me live my life over
once again, once again.
Once again, take me back to those wide open spaces
where a friend is a friend, and where a pal is a pal
all along, all along.*

THE MOST FAMOUS HERO OF THE WEST

WILLIAM L. BOYD

IN THOSE HAPPY DAYS OF YOUTH, a wonderful thing used to happen every Saturday morning — some 60 years ago or so. I remember going to the local movie house, shelling out my hard earned dime and entering a world of excitement and adventure. After standing in line to get my ticket and once inside, I'd head for the snack bar for a Coke and a box of popcorn and then I'd be off to find a good seat.

A handsome publicity shot of both hero and steed from **Call of the Prairie** *(1936).*

When the theater lights dimmed, the curtains would part, and the show would begin. Sometimes there were previews of the coming attractions, a cartoon and a serial chapter. Then there would be the main attraction of the day. Hopalong Cassidy, Lucky Jenkins and California Carlson would ride across that screen in another great exciting western adventure.

In those happy days of youth, with a good Hopalong Cassidy western, I was in a world of my own. For about 60 minutes, I was totally involved with the cowboy star as he corralled the outlaws, the stagecoach bandit and the bank robbers. And on top of that, the Bar-20 boys could still find time to round up the cattle rustlers and take care of a claim jumper.

At that time, some of my best friends were cowboys: Allan "Rocky" Lane with his stallion Black Jack, Tex Ritter and White Flash, Red Ryder and his horse Thunder, Ken Maynard and Tarzan, Charles Starrett aka "The Durango Kid" and his steed Raider, and Hopalong Cassidy and his beautiful white stallion Topper.

I knew them all and they were as real to me as my own family. I loved those cowboys and those western movies,

Scene from **Rustler's Valley** *(1937).*

CLARENCE E. MULFORD'S

LUMBERJACK

FEATURING

WILLIAM BOYD

as Hopalong Cassidy

with JIMMY ROGERS · ANDY CLYDE

DOUGLASS DUMBRILLE ELLEN HALL

FRANCIS McDONALD

Directed by LESLEY SELANDER · A HARRY SHERMAN Production

Released thru MASTERPIECE Productions

PRODUCTIONS

and I still do even today. I have fond memories of sitting around the campfire with all my cowboy heroes of the BAR-20 after a hard day of rounding up the strays. I have even rode alongside Rex Allen and his horse Koko, with Monte Hale and Partner, and Johnny Mack Brown and his faithful horse Rebel. Yes, the West was a wonderful place in those happy youthful days.

The happiest days of my youth were the Saturdays when my hero, Hopalong Cassidy was going to be playing at the local movie house. It meant I was going to see Hopalong Cassidy and his beautiful white horse Topper and all my saddle pals from the Bar-20 Ranch. Hopalong Cassidy, Lucky Jenkins, California Carlson, Red Conners and Buck Peters. They would all be there ready again for another great western adventure. You knew when those good guys saddled up to ride, the outlaw's days were numbered. On those wonderful Saturday afternoons when you left the movie theatre after a Hopalong Cassidy movie, you had a good feeling and you knew the world was a better place.

Andy Clyde (left) and Jay Kirby (not Jimmy Rodgers, as credited on card) and Hoppy in scene from another film was mistakenly placed onto card. Movie card for **Lumberjack** *(1944).*

HOPALONG CASSIDY!

If you were interested in westerns, either in print or on film, at any time from 1905 till the middle-50's, the name Hopalong Cassidy meant something. Between 1905 and the mid-1930's, the name described the red headed, tobacco spitting, limping Arthurian knight who was the main character in a long series of novels and short stories written by Clarence E. Mulford.

From 1935 through the late-40's, it meant the silver-haired, black-dressed hero of the saddle. The most famous hero of the West was galloping across the nation's movie screens on his white horse Topper.

From 1949 until the middle-to-late-50's the name meant the premier cowboy star of the early years of commercial TV. Hoppy was the first TV super star. Since then the name has been almost forgotten…but not forgotten by all.

The best of the Hopalong Cassidy movies are among the finest western series ever made. When seen complete and uncut, they are a joy to watch today as they were sixty

years ago. But chances are they will never be seen again on the big screen by large audiences the way they were meant to be seen. After watching some of Hoppy's movies from my collection (which consist of all 66 movies that were made), I found that the good ones were even better than I remembered them to be. Judged on acting ability you would have to put Bill Boyd at the top of the list of B-Western Cowboy actors. William Boyd had been acting for fifteen years, before he started playing the role of Clarence E. Mulford's Hopalong Cassidy.

Unlike the comic book character, Red Ryder, played in the movie westerns by four different stars; (Don "Red" Barry, Allan Lane, Jim Bannon and Bill Elliott), William Boyd was the only actor to play Hopalong Cassidy — in sixty-six feature films (the most films ever made by an actor playing the same character).

Boyd broke into the movies in 1919. In 1920, he was an extra in Cecil B. DeMille's film called *Why Change Your Wife*. DeMille instantly noticed the star quality in Boyd, a handsome rugged blonde. He was quickly elevated to supporting roles and later to leading-man roles. He appeared in such films as *The Volga Boatman*, *King of Kings* and *Two Arabian Nights*. Boyd became a romantic idol in the

*Publicity pose for **Three on the Trail** (1936) with James Ellison as "Johnny Nelson" (left) and George "Gabby" Hayes as "Windy Halliday."*

AS THRILLING AS THE WEST ITSELF...
AS GREAT AS ONLY
MITCHUM CAN BE !
MASTERPIECE PRODUCTIONS present
FALSE COLORS
Starring
BOB MITCHUM
WILLIAM BOYD
WITH
ANDY CLYDE · JIMMY ROGERS
DOUGLASS DUMBRILLE
DIRECTED BY GEORGE ARCHAINBAUD
Screenplay by BENNET COHEN · Based on
characters created by CLARENCE E. MULFORD
A HARRY SHERMAN production
Released thru MASTERPIECE PRODUCTIONS
MASTERPIECE PRODUCTIONS

1920's — in a class with Wallace Reid and Rod LaRocque. The era of sound was a mixed blessing for William Boyd. Unlike many of his peers, he successfully made the transition to talkies. Dazzled by success, he spent freely, gambled heavy and lived lavishly. But in 1932 Boyd's good life came to a screeching halt.

Unfortunately there was another William Boyd — a Broadway actor — who was arrested at a drinking and gambling party. In the morning Hollywood newspapers, Mr. William L. Boyd's picture was published in error. An apology was printed later, but Boyd's career plunged downhill. The mistaken identity had made things very hard on Boyd and soon he began going by Bill Boyd. However, there was another Bill Boyd who appeared in low budget, singing cowboy westerns and billed himself as "The Cowboy Rambler."

Finally, in 1935, William L. Boyd gained his own famous identity as Hopalong Cassidy. His first Hoppy movie was entitled *Hop-A-Long Cassidy*. It was released on July 30, 1935 and was based on Mulford's 1910 novel by the same name.

*Theater card for **False Colors** (1943) with a young "Bob" Mitchum as "Rip Austin" getting top billing.*

Boyd said that until 1935 that he had a dual personality. "I had a good side and a bad side. I fought the bad side but I couldn't win. Then I became Hopalong Cassidy and the good side took over and I lost the Bill Boyd identity and I'm grateful I did."

Although I never met William Boyd, the unforgettable star of the series, I had the privilege of meeting his widow, Grace Bradley Boyd. And after talking with Grace, about our favorite subject, "Hoppy," I knew, as a kid growing up, I had the greatest childhood hero a kid could've had. Hopalong Cassidy was the Sir Galahad of the range, a soft spoken paragon who did not smoke, drink, or kiss the girls, who tried to capture the rustlers instead of shooting them, and who always let the villain draw first if it came to gun play. Never in the history of Hollywood has one man played the same character in so many features. When audiences all over the world saw the Hoppy films, Bill Boyd and Hopalong Cassidy became synonymous. The two greatest things that ever happened to William L. Boyd were "Grace Bradley" and "Hopalong Cassidy." Grace was the perfect partner for Boyd, and Hopalong Cassidy was the ideal character for Boyd to play.

 Notice: for authenticity, the guns had bullets in them.

Although he was born William Lawrence Boyd on June 5th 1895, the son of a construction worker, he was known to millions of youngsters — as he galloped across the silver screen between 1935 and 1948 on his beautiful white stallion Topper — simply as "Hoppy." Hoppy rode with ruggedly handsome pals Russell Hayden, Jimmy Ellison and durable sidekicks George "Gabby" Hayes and Andy Clyde (who played "California Carlson" and co-starred with Hoppy in 1940 in *Three Men From Texas* and would be Hoppy's sidekick through 1948 when the last Hopalong Cassidy theater western *Strange Gamble* was released in October of that year.) Clad in a black hat, atop his white mount Topper, along with his hardy laugh and rugged-but-gentle protectiveness, William Boyd captured the fertile imagination and loving hearts of an innocent generation who came to worship their hero on Saturday mornings in the 1940's!

The Hopalong Cassidy film series started in 1935 with William Boyd as Hopalong Cassidy and Harry "Pop" Sherman as the producer. After nine years and producing some of the best westerns of the time, Sherman wanted out because a few years before the Hopalong Cassidy films had become a box-office disaster. But it was William Boyd who turned failure into a phenomenon.

There are those great rocks in the background.

After June 23, 1944, when *Forty Thieves* was released, Boyd was an actor without a series because no new Hoppy films would be made released until *The Devil's Playground* debuted in November of 1946. It was the first Hoppy movie produced by the William Boyd Production Company.

Boyd went on the road becoming an attraction for the Cole's Bros. Circus that toured the country. His salary: $250 per week. Finally, in 1946 he found a promoter by the name of Toby Anguish who agreed that there was a future in the Hopalong Cassidy westerns. But after lining up investors, the promoter discovered that they needed to purchase the rights to the character from Harry Sherman who, even though he had abandoned the series, still continued to pay an annual fee to Clarence E. Mulford. Boyd himself approached the veteran producer to cut a deal. Sherman thought he was kidding since he considered the Cassidy property to be box-office death.

Sherman was convinced of Boyd's seriousness — especially when he paid $250,000 cash for the rights to produce new Hoppy features. The deal also included rights to the fifty-four Hoppy films produced by Sherman. William Boyd Productions was formed. But as Sherman predicted,

Great publicity shot of Russell Hayden and Gabby Hayes with our hero.

1688-

the new series of twelve Hoppy films failed at the box offices. It looked as though both Cassidy and Boyd were finished in the movie business. Boyd and Anguish made one last desperate gamble. Together, they went deeply in debt to premier Hoppy in the experimental medium of television.

In the late 1940's there was little of any true quality on television. The major studios considered it competition. Boyd edited down the Cassidy features to fit a 60-minute-time-frame and *Hopalong Cassidy* premiered as a weekly series in November of 1948. Right from the start the Hoppy series scored high ratings. NBC was impressed and cut a deal to move the Cassidy show into prime time. Hopalong Cassidy became one of the TV media's first super stars. Suddenly, to millions of children, Hopalong Cassidy became their hero. The risky venture had paid off and Bill Boyd became an over-night millionaire.

Everyone loved Hoppy! Thus in the 1950's, Hopalong Cassidy was a well chosen ambassador of man's noble virtues for a new generation, a symbol of justice and honor in an age tarnished by unjust border wars, unresolved police actions, unsettling cold-war confrontations and acute totalitarian expansion! In such a formless, chaotic

 The handsome sidekick, Russell Hayden.

period, knights of chivalry, heroes, guardians of peace and leaders of vision were surprisingly rare and decidedly needed! Although fictitious, the legendary cowboy in black **was such a man**. Boyd founded a club called *Hoppy's Troopers* and its membership rivaled that of the Boy Scouts of America. It had a *Hopalong Code of Conduct*, which preached loyalty, honesty, ambition, kindness and other virtues. To millions of impressionable youngsters, Hoppy was a hero, protector, defender of the trail — a path of HONOR, EQUALITY and FAIR PLAY on which each of us was expected to travel! William Boyd donated money to children's hospitals and homes, saying: "The way I figure it, if it weren't for the kids, I'd be a bum today. They're the ones who've made my success possible and they should benefit from it."

Once in a great while an actor's role as a certain character will so overshadow his other cinematic accomplishments and even his given name, that to the whole world he becomes that character. Such was the case with William Boyd, once he took the role of Clarence E. Mulford's drifting two-gun cowpoke Hopalong Cassidy. A striking black clad figure, astride a beautiful white horse named Topper, Hoppy rode through the old west righting wrongs, helping the down-and-out, rescuing the rancher's

Tournament of Roses Parade with a proud Bill Ross standing with his buddy Hoppy (notice the Michigan float in the backround).

daughter, and sending evildoers scurrying for their holes. He didn't drink or smoke, seldom got angry and always let the villains draw first, preferring to wound them instead of gunning them down.

William Boyd didn't like the coldness of the Hoppy character in the early films and he eventually played the character the way he felt portrayed him best. He avoided playing stupid cowpokes that said "purty" and "ain't" and "they went that-a-way." He had Hoppy speak intelligently and use his wits.

There are countless sod-busters and buckaroos who, consciously, have never been side-tracked or bush-whacked along life's righteous path — and Hoppy would be proud of any contribution he might have made to making that happen. From his example we learned courage, decency, honor and respect — sterling characteristics, ideally structured and synthesized in the formulation of a child's behavior! Such was his legacy; such was the man. William Boyd as Hopalong Cassidy still evokes the memory of last roundups, faded sunsets and heroes past! But, more importantly Hoppy remains a constant symbol of our most noble virtues!

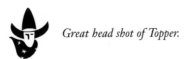 *Great head shot of Topper.*

Grace told me that the first time she saw Hoppy she fell in love with him. After meeting in Hollywood in 1937, three weeks later they were married. They were only apart two times in their marriage of thirty-five years. Both occasions involved Grace leaving movie locations, where Hoppy was shooting films, to return home to decorate their house for Christmas. Grace Bradley was a star of stage and screen but considers her role as "Mrs. Hoppy" the most rewarding of all. Hoppy and Grace: they were "The Perfect Couple."

Grace Bradley was born in Brooklyn. She performed her first concert piano recital at the age of six, and at the age of twelve she won a two year scholarship to the Eastern School of Dance. Grace appeared on Broadway and later in movies. Her first movie was *To Much Harmony with Bing Crosby*.

Grace and Hoppy, as was stated earlier, spent only two nights apart in their thirty-five years of marriage. Grace said, "I never went to bed before him and I never got up after him. Hoppy was absolutely the most handsome man you ever saw, with those china blue eyes, black brows and skin like a baby. He was 6-feet tall and everything was per-

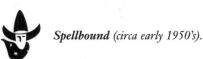
Spellbound (circa early 1950's).

fectly in proportion. I had to fight the women off with a club. They swarmed all over him." Very much in love with one another, Grace constantly found love notes all over the house.

Grace's horse and riding outfit were her first Christmas gifts from William Boyd. Her horse was named Turnabout. In 1937, when Bill married Grace, he also acquired a new white stallion. He asked Grace to name the horse. At the time, Grace was reading a series of books called *Topper*. Grace asked Bill to name the horse after her favorite book...and that's how Topper got his name.

Grace and Hoppy married on Hoppy's birthday: June 5th, 1937. At the time of the marriage Hoppy was shooting a new movie on location in Lone Pine entitled *Hopalong Rides Again*. They stayed in a small cabin on location and still stands there today. You have seen it many times in a lot of the old western movies. The cabin was, and is today, referred to as the Hoppy Cabin.

Grace asked me when I first became a Hoppy fan. At the age of five or six, I saw Hoppy for the first time on his beautiful white horse and I was hooked on Hopalong Cassidy from that time on.

THE MOST FAMOUS HERO OF THE WEST

In order to see my first movie, I did some small jobs helping gentlemen that owned a small grocery store down the road from our family's house. I saved the pennies and nickels I earned that week. On Saturday morning, I told my mom I was going to the movie with Bob, a friend that lived down the road from us. I was told to come straight home after the movie. The movie that week was a Hopalong Cassidy movie — the first movie I had ever seen. So after watching it a couple of times, Bob wanted to go home. But I was enjoying this new experience too much to leave. Bob left to go home but, I stayed and watched Hoppy over and over, again and again.

When I finally left the theater, it was so dark and I was scared to death. I had to walk down a long, dark road to get home and cross over a creek on an old swinging bridge. All my fear left me for a few minutes, when I spotted my stepfather. But after he got a little closer, I could see that he was not in a good frame of mind. He was carrying a switch about three or four feet long. He started to use it on me, and he continued all the way home — except when we had to cross that swinging bridge. I have to say that switching left a impression on me for a long time — not to mention the marks on my back, my legs and my behind. If a parent did that today to a kid, they would lock

29

*Scene from **Bar 20** (1943) with sidekick Andy Clyde standing between Hoppy and Robert Mitchum along with Dustine Farnum and Betty Blythe.*

them up and throw away the key. It hurt for a while, but it didn't kill me and I never pulled a trick like that again. But you know...it was all worth it. For a whole day, and part of a night, I got to ride with Hopalong Cassidy, Lucky Jenkins and California Carlson. What an adventure that was — one I never forgot. Hoppy and Topper, Lucky and California on a big theater screen...it being the first movie I had ever seen: What more could a kid want?

The Hopalong Cassidy movie I saw that day, ***Three Men From Texas***, also left a lasting impression on me — no wonder I must have watched it six or seven times. It's the first time Hoppy meets up with California who becomes his partner through out the rest of Hoppy's run in the pro- duced-for-theater movies. It is one of the better Hoppy movies and is one of my favorites. This Hoppy movie, along with that switching I got that night by my stepfa- ther, left a lasting impression on me. Hoppy, my favorite hero of the old West left an impression on me that has lasted a lifetime.

If after that night, I had known the way to San Jose I would have run away from home...maybe to Arizona and a visit to the Bar-20 Ranch...and then maybe on to California, with a sure stop over at **Hoppyland** — the

 Bill Boyd and his perfect partner, Grace Bradley.

Hopalong Cassidy amusement park at 400 Washington St. in Venice, CA. **Hoppyland** was an eighty acre site with picnic grounds, a baseball field (where I surely would have found my *Field of Dreams*), a horseshoe-pitching area, and more than 20 thrill rides. Boat races and water-ski shows were held on the 17-acre Lake Los Angeles. William Boyd made regular appearances at the park. **Hoppyland** opened May 27, 1951 (four years before **Disneyland**) and it closed its doors in 1954 as Hoppy Mania began to fizzle out. The height of the Hoppy craze was 1952 when Hoppy merchandising garnered over $70 million dollars. Hoppy had hundreds of products that he endorsed everything from **Bond** bread to radios.

Boyd rose to the challenge of being "The Most Famous Hero Of The West" and became quite a proficient wrangler and rider — thanks to his faithful companion, Topper, who remained with him for 19 years. Hopalong Cassidy's philosophy of clean living, non-smoking, sobriety, and swearing carried over into Boyd's private life.

His blonde hair had soon turned completely silver adding more distinction to his persona. Boyd made fifty-four Hopalong Cassidy movies from 1935 to 1943 — all produced by Harry "Pop" Sherman. In 1943 Boyd took over

Grace wearing the lst-anniversary present from Bill — matching outfits.

the reigns of producer and made twelve more Hopalong Cassidy films.

When television dawned, Bill "Hopalong" Boyd was there. Within a year, NBC had paid Boyd a quarter of a million dollars for the weekly presentation of the Hopalong Cassidy movies. Within two years, Hoppy appeared in a comic strip that was syndicated by the *Los Angeles Times*. He was seen in over 15 million comic books that first year. 50 million records were sold in the first month. More than fifty products featured the cowboy's regalia. He became wealthy exhibiting his old films on his own television show and marketing the tie-in products. The merchandising included Hopalong Cassidy lunch boxes, pajamas, wallpaper, bicycles (with handlebars shaped like steer horns and a spot for a six shooter on the frame), cookies, pocket knives, watches, compasses, hair cream, toothpaste, records, guns, hats, chaps, books, belts, candy bars, peanut butter, and roller skates with spurs. Hoppy also had a gum company, but Boyd would not license his bubble gum. By 1950 Hoppy was seen on 63 TV stations and heard on one hundred-and-fifty-two radio outlets. One hundred-and-fifty-five newspapers carried his adventures in their comic sections. William Boyd got rich from Hopalong Cassidy by having the foresight and the wisdom to buy the TV rights to the films in the

 Not many cowboys could wear that hat and look that good.

1940's. As a result, Hopalong Cassidy became the first TV cowboy hero!

The *New York Daily News* ran the comic strip for the first time on Wednesday January 4, 1950 with an announcement inviting all to meet Hopalong Cassidy in person at the News Building Saturday at 2 P.M. Early estimates were that 50,000 people would show. Extravagant estimates were set at 100,000. The actual turnout exceeded 350,000. Hopalong Cassidy, riding shotgun in a Cadillac convertible, rode up 42nd Street to the News Building. Hoppy, seeing the extent of the crowd, vowed: "I'll stay rooted here until every last hand is shaken." He stayed. From 2 P.M., until after dark, he greeted New York.

Hoppy shook hands, touched or kissed each person. Some were kids. Some were women. The crowd moved past Hoppy to a location where thirty men busily dug into cartons to hand out Hoppy buttons and paper click-guns. The day was cold and windy, but this was a happy crowd. Four hundred of New York's finest were on hand to keep order, but it wasn't a difficult job because the crowd (larger than the population of Cincinnati at the time) was having fun...a party. Kids were dressed in their cowboy suits pulled over winter clothing. Some families brought

Scene from Three Men From Texas (1940) with Russell Hayden as "Lucky Jenkins" and Andy Clyde as "California Carlson."

lunches for them and the kids. Thousands of others looked at the line, became discouraged and turned away.

Those who stayed were four, five, six-abreast for several blocks, but closer to the News Building the line bulged to fifteen abreast. Floodlights were set up to brighten the street after nightfall. The lines continued to pass Hoppy until the last hand had been shaken and the last person had been greeted.

For weeks after Hoppy left town, kids were still coming to the News Building lobby — over 400 an hour — to pick up a Hopalong Cassidy souvenir button.

Interestingly, Bill Boyd had tried for months to sell the comic strip to a rival newspaper without success. When the *Daily News* began running it, the staff anticipated a circulation increase of 50,000 within six months. However, reality was even better than expected: the very next day sales jumped by 87,000 with another 10,000 the second day. The rival newspaper publisher threatened to blast Boyd in print because he had put the comic strip in the *Daily News*. Boyd countered by presenting a letter from an executive of the rival paper, dated a couple of

years earlier, which summarily rejected the whole comic strip idea thus ending the matter.

By 1950 nearly all western pictures had ceased being made by the studios, but the "Hoppies" were still going strong. The name *Hoppy* had become a household word and the market was being flooded with different products using the name and likeness of this star. At one time there was nearly two hundred different items relating to the western cowboy star — items from radios to hair tonic. The most cherished items today are the Hopalong Cassidy comic books, lobby cards, and one-sheets that are being sold at handsome prices by numerous movie memorabilia collectors.

The Hoppy craze lasted about ten years and left the Boyd's wealthy beyond one's dream. Bill's last screen appearance was for the same studio that released his first Hoppy series, Paramount. Bill played himself in a cameo role for his one-time boss, Cecil B. DeMille, in *The Greatest Show On Earth*. One might say that Bill had made the perfect circle to where it all began.

Bill's health began failing in the 1960's and at one point, interviews were discontinued. His physical appearance

One rare movie promo shot (great shadow effect).

BOYD

had changed so that he didn't want his fans to see him in that condition. "I would rather they remember me as they saw me on the screen," was Bill's solemn remark. Who could ever forget the greatest western hero of all time? No one!

From the moment *Hopalong Cassidy* premiered on NBC, Bill Boyd became an international hero. The films were telecast not only in America but all over the world. His popularity was astounding. He received over 15,000 fan letters a week. He received endless and persistent requests from individuals and international organizations to make public appearances.

He made two worldwide tours while NBC was pressing him to continue production. The stress was tremendous. He was in his sixties at this time, and he felt that the Hoppy character could not be properly portrayed at that age. He also was feeling the pressure of being in front of the cameras month after month, week after week. The year before he retired, he made forty Hoppy episodes in forty weeks and made one more tour around the world for the Newsboys' Association.

Unusual shot of Hoppy sans guns and holsters.

After completing that tour, Hoppy put Topper out to pasture, hung up his guns, took off his boots, and said adios to Hopalong Cassidy, his alter ego. CBS was about to start shooting the series, *Gunsmoke* at that time, and Boyd was able to turn over his company to the network, assuring employment for his entire crew.

Bill Boyd's television success has never been rivaled. During his public appearances, as many as a million fans turned out to see him. These fans included presidents, senators, congressmen, governors, mayors, admirals, generals, ambassadors, prime ministers, and of course the public.

Boyd didn't sing, dance, play football, baseball or basketball, nor did he box, play tennis or race cars. Boyd was merely Hopalong Cassidy. He smiled, waved, shook hands, and had that contagious laugh. He was simply Mr. Good Guy — everybody's favorite cowboy — Friend, Buddy, Pal — **The Most Famous Hero Of The West**.

William L. Boyd retired from active show business in 1953, after sixty-six feature films, one hundred-and-four radio shows and fifty-two television shows. William Boyd lived the rest of his years with his beautiful, charming wife

Hoppy photo autographed by Grace Bradley Boyd ("Mrs. Hopalong Cassidy").

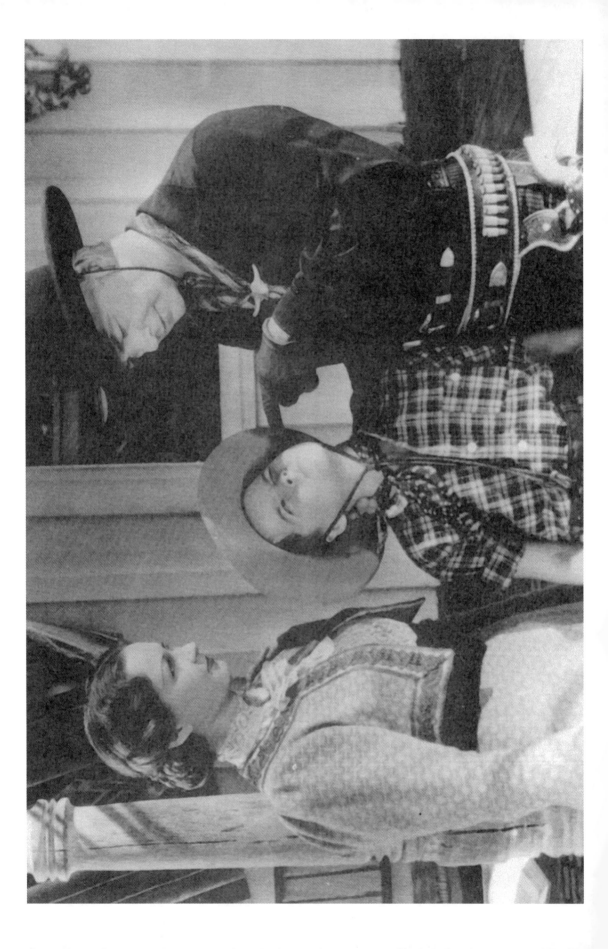

Grace Bradley Boyd. Bob Stabler, the general manager of William Boyd Enterprises and Hopalong Cassidy, Inc., his wife Dorothy, and the Boyds traveled extensively together around the world to scheduled events and promotional tours. Dorothy Stabler noticed that the relationship between Bob Stabler and Bill Boyd was more like a father and son relationship, tumultuous, but devoted.

Dorothy and Grace would attend parades that featured Hoppy. They would stand alongside parade routes and wave as Hopalong rode by astride Topper. Topper would recognize Grace's voice as she yelled from the crowd, "Hey Topper!" Topper would come to a stop in the parade and look around for her.

Hoppy spent the last few months of his life in the South Coast Medical Center in Laguna Beach, CA. While Hoppy was there, Grace had a cot brought into the room at the hospital and never left his side. After his death Grace became a medical center volunteer assisting in all areas of the hospital. Every Christmas she made the rounds — visiting hospital patients.

In 1972, the young kids of America lost a true hero. William Boyd became so identified with his screen char-

Little Dickie Jones with Elelyn Venable in **The Frontiersman** *(1938).*

acter that he became that character in the minds of his fans. William Boyd had insisted that Hoppy never smoke, cuss or do anything that might detract from the positive image associated with him in the minds of the youth of America.

William Boyd passed into legend at the age of seventy-seven in 1972. The character however lives on in the videos of his feature films and his television episodes. You could never finish writing about all the good and remarkable things this man accomplished. He was one-of-a-kind. I only wish there were some like him around today to hold up before America's youth!

What the youth of America need today is to discover the heroes from those wonderful days gone by — when Hoppy, Roy and Gene rode across our silver screens. ONCE AGAIN, WE NEED TO LIVE IN GOD'S COUNTRY... WE DON'T LIVE THERE ANYMORE! OH! WHAT I'D GIVE JUST TO LIVE IN GOD'S COUNTRY, ONCE AGAIN...BACK THEN!

But in life, all good things have to come to an end...Hop-a-long...Cas-si-dy...Hop-a-long...there he goes...Down the moonlit trail...but he'll return....soon again...no need

Sheriff's Rodeo (circa early 1950's) with co-hosts Hoppy and a young Debbie Reynolds.

to say goodbye...until then...So-long Hopalong...So-long ...till we meet again!

Thanks for the Memories!

Hoppy

For The Exciting Adventures In My Happy Days of Youth

The strong image remembered by loyal fans around the world.

CHAPTER 2

ACTION HERO OF THE WEST

ALLEN "ROCKY" LANE

THE MOST FAMOUS ACTION HERO of the West was as a fellow by the name of Allen "Rocky" Lane. Allen's pictures were always full of fast action and had good stories to back up the fisticuffs and hard riding in which Rocky engaged. Like all the B-Western Stars, Allen had his own special horse in all of his movies. Allen's horse was "Black Jack" — almost as famous as Allen himself. Black Jack had his own page in the back of the Rocky Lane Western comic books. It was called "Black Jack's Hitching Post." It featured, not surprisingly, information on horses.

*Theater card for **Salt Lake Raiders** (1950) that featured a young Martha Hyer as "Helen Thornton."*

This western star featured fast action in all his movies. Action was the keynote in the Rocky Lane pictures. His imposing physical presence became one of his most popular characteristics. Allen looked more like a pro athlete than a movie star.

The road to outdoor western pictures wasn't a simple or easy one for Allen Lane. During his first years in the movies he played leading men in drawing-room dramas and light comedies, but it was Allen's hope that in time he could eventually make it into westerns. After making appearances in a couple of westerns, Republic Studios signed Allan to western pictures exclusively. Fans agreed with Allan, that in action westerns he was at his best and his popularity with the movie-going crowds proved they liked pictures with hard riding and quick shooting.

For a long time before becoming an Action-Ace Cowboy, Rocky Lane appeared in the movies as Alan Lane, a well-muscled hero of polite dramas opposite actresses such as Joan Fontaine and Ginger Rogers. He was not happy with his lot in those drawing-room dramas and roles in light comedy.

Great pose by the former football player and model with Black Jack.

1718-

The son of an Indiana farmer, he visited the New Mexico ranch of some relatives when he was seven years old. He was captivated by the west and dreamed of being a cowboy. Back in Indiana, he dreamed of being a cowboy, and after finishing his schooling, he made tracks for the West. While attending a rodeo he was spotted, signed and hauled into those Hollywood drawing-room scenes.

About to leave town in disgust, Lane was offered his first role as a cowboy role. That fixed it for him and he stayed on, starring in westerns as the six-foot plus, husky-built Allan "Rocky" Lane. He worked overtime to make himself a worthy cowboy and became proud of his riding, roping and bulldogging talents.

He lived in the San Fernando Valley in a home decorated in manly leather and wood. It was filled with western decor. Shelves in his bedroom closet were stacked with ten-gallon hats and the floor of the closet was littered with boots. He made up for lost time by wearing nothing but cowboy clothes and riding his stallion Black Jack whenever possible.

Rocky was one of the few Saturday afternoon cowboys who never went in for singing and playing a guitar, even

 Pals

though he had a very fine voice. He went in for the rough, tough, action-packed films that had lots of shooting and scrapping — the real *he-man* stuff.

His films always featured a hard riding character, who saw to it that right always prevailed. Rocky felt if you were right and fought hard you would win. He was chafed by the restrictions imposed by Republic Studios that prohibited him from competing in rodeos because of the physical danger they posed. Allan liked the rough, tough thrills of rodeos and the cowboy life they represented.

Of the various aspects of western life, Allan loved guns and shooting in particular. He owned dozens of firearms — many of them authentic relics of pioneer days — and kept them around his bachelor home. It didn't take much of a hint to get him to drag a guest out the back door and start popping away at a target set up in the trees in his back yard.

In 1946, Bill Elliott abandoned the **Red Ryder** series, after making sixteen films. He had hopes of making larger-budget westerns — more or less like the John Wayne-type films. The **Red Ryder** series then was taken over by Allan Lane but still featured Bobby Blake as Little Beaver.

 Studio publicity pose (great teeth!).

The Lane-Ryder and the Elliott-Ryder series, were the best Red Ryder movies made and they were good money-makers for the theater owners. The series gave Allan "Rocky" Lane the exposure to the Saturday afternoon moviegoers that he needed to make him a top-ten draw at the box-office.

Fans are mixed on their Red Ryder preferences. Don "Red" Barry was well liked in the role, but he was a one-time star in the Red Ryder serial. Another star who had no appeal at all as Red Ryder was Jim Bannon. Lane's youth-fulness (compared to Elliott) appealed to many. One could feel the "older-brother relationship" with Little Beaver, and it played better than Bill Eilliott's fatherly figure. Some fans liked the more forceful character that Bill Elliott brought to the role. The real difference came down to the individual actor's personalities and which appealed to the fans.

Republic Studios gave Allan Lane the same production quality and strong casts that had been available to Bill Elliott. The one change I personally didn't like was the recasting of the Duchess Role. Alice Fleming had made such a strong impression on the Red Ryder fans during the sixteen Elliott-Ryder films that Martha Wentworth could never quite claim the role for her own.

 *Publicity shot for **Salt Lake Raiders** (1950).*

Following the memorable stint as the range-hardened Red Ryder, Allan Lane began his most famous series for Republic Studios. Making thirty-two action-packed western adventures firmly established Rocky as a top-ten cowboy star — and a household name from then on.

Republic studios: Why? Why did you wait so long? Look at what we lost. There should have been a lot more films of Allan "Rocky" Lane for us to have seen and enjoyed at our local movie houses each Saturday — not to mention all the other films we would have to watch today on video.

What was most impressive about Rocky was how his handsome good looks were accentuated when he rode his beautiful black horse (the coat on Black Jack seemed to shine like a silver dollar). Rocky Lane was one of the most handsome of all the cowboy stars — especially in his pinstriped shirt and plain old blue jeans. The idea of wearing jeans was a good one. It made him all the more appealing in many ways. He topped off his wardrobe with the greatest looking white hat one would ever want to own.

Yes, Rocky was what every boy wished to be. Sitting on Black Jack, no one could compare. He always looked good in riding scenes. I loved the way he rode Black Jack from

Taken from color photo shot on location by member of crew.

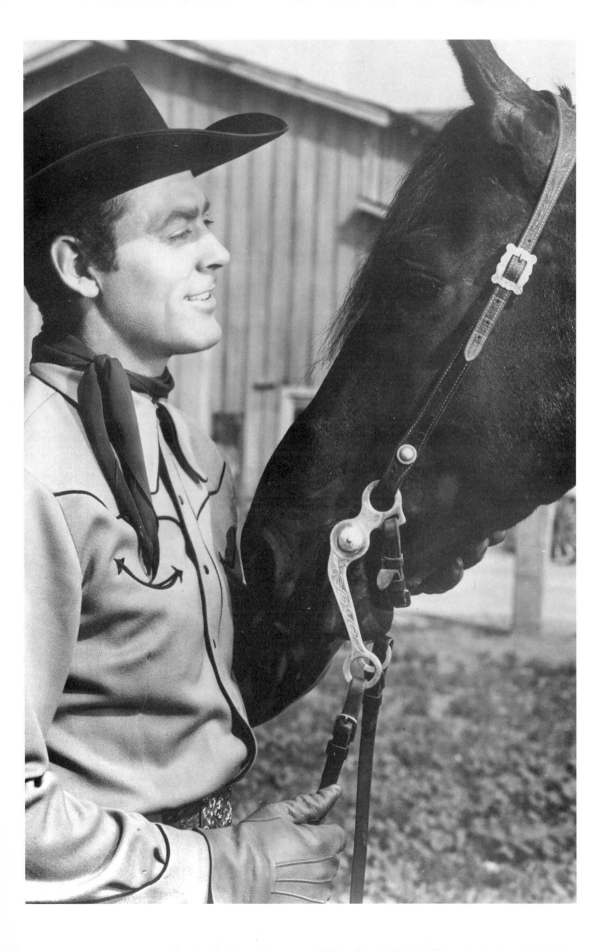

a gallop to a sudden stop (Black Jack looked like he had air brakes the way he could stop in a split second). I also got a thrill at the way Rocky could slide head first on his stomach into the camera as he headed for cover from the bad-guy's bullets. Rocky could slide head first, almost as good as Pete Rose going into second base. Great action, I really loved those scenes as a kid — still do. Guess I haven't drifted too far from *Those Wide Open Spaces*, for I still love a good Rocky Lane western.

The Allan "Rocky" Lane movies I have and watch from time to time, are as thoroughly enjoyable as they were back then in the 40's and 50's. Being a Hopalong Cassidy and an Allan "Rocky" Lane fan often makes me feel that somehow I got cheated. When it comes to Rocky Lane, Republic should have done it sooner, bigger, and better with a whole lot more Allan "Rocky" Lane product.

All of the good B-Western cowboy stars had great sidekicks and Rocky Lane was no exception. Eddy Waller was the perfect sidekick for the usually sober-sided Rocky Lane. Eddy as Nugget Clark could provide gentle humorous scenes or he could get involved with the action in a serious and believable manner.

Eddy Waller who often portrayed "Nugget Clark".

Eddy Waller came to Hollywood in 1936, as a character actor, worked regularly in the movies and television until about 1960. He died at the age of eighty-eight in 1977. He is probably best remembered for his role as Nugget Clark. The first western movie I remember seeing Eddy Waller appear in was a 1941 Hopalong Cassidy adventure called *In Old Colorado*.

Eddy Waller first entered show business at the age of fourteen, much against the wishes of his preacher father. After two years on the stage his parents bribed him into quitting by offering to pay his way through college. His longing for the stage brought him back to Broadway after graduation.

I wonder how a fine actor like Eddy Waller could have worked with Allan "Rocky" Lane for so long, considering those directors, producers, other stars and stagehands supposedly disliked him so much. At least some of the Hollywood types would have you believe that was the case. Eddy Waller once stated, "I got along fine with Rocky Lane. If someone met with misfortune, Rocky would give them his last dollar. He was always a compassionate person." I prefer to believe what Eddy Waller and Walter Reed thought of Rocky.

Lane and Waller in studio publicity shot (note drop screen in background).

Walter Reed, who was once a RKO Studios contract player, became a serial hero at Republic Studios where Rocky
Lane was under contract. Walter Reed was also a screen
and later-TV heavy opposite such stars as Tim Holt,
Annie Oakley, Clint Walker, Randolph Scott, and Rocky
Lane. Reed also worked in several John Ford films. All of
the films were true professional works, and looking at the
end result, they could be considered perfection.

Walter Reed would say of Rocky Lane: "Rocky had a reputation for being hard to work with, but let me tell you, he
was a perfectionist. Many times after we got through
working for the day, we would go have a drink together,
and he was one of the nicest guys you would ever want to
meet. He liked working with experienced people. It was
his series, and he wanted it to be good."

Rocky Lane was not born a cowboy — he became a cowboy. Once he got his horse Black Jack, he learned to be a
superior rider. He started to wear Levi's in his western
movies and all the kids in school started wearing them –
turning them up at the bottom just like Rocky Lane. We
could have cared less if Rocky was not popular with the
actors, directors, and production crews on the sets at
Republic Pictures. He was a popular among all of his fans

– those that filled the theaters every Saturday when his westerns were playing. We, the loyal Allen "Rocky" Lane fans, were the ones who bought the tickets, the popcorn, candy, and sodas at the snack bar. We were the ones who counted most and we, the fans, loved our "Action hero of the West" – Allen "Rocky" Lane!

During the 1940's and early 1950's we sat with our eyes glued to the silver screen as he rode a beautiful black stallion named Thunder. As Red Ryder, and later in his own series, he rode that other beautiful black stallion, Black Jack, as he *thwarted* the bad guy. And more often than not, it would be that number one black-hat villain of them all: Roy Barcroft.

Since Allan Lane was a hero to us — the Saturday matinee fans, the ones that bought the tickets and made him a star — what you (Mr. Yakima, Mr. Coffin, Mr. Frost, Mr. Witney, and Mr. Springsteen) thought of him does not matter even a little bit. Just maybe you guys never spent enough time with him personally to get to know him, getting to know the man that he really was — not the play-acting western cowboy star.

Why would one performer want to knock another fellow actor? I believe there is another side to this matter that we

Relaxing with Roy Rogers.

have not heard. If you can't say something good about someone, why say anything at all. I'm a die-hard — always was and always will be — true-blue Hopalong Cassidy fan. And I will be the first to admit that Allan "Rocky" Lane played the B-Western cowboy role better — or as good as anyone that ever rode across the silver screen.

His fans must have thought so as well, because every Saturday when a Rocky Lane movie was playing at the State Theater back home in Kentucky, we would pack 'em in and do a great snack bar business. The action was equally as fast at the snack bar as it was on the screen. It was always a great day all around when Rocky came to town! Rocky and Nugget came riding down our trail one last time in the movie *El Paso Stampede*. It was in this film that Rocky and Nugget would have their last shoot out with the bad guys.

We all know that in every western in which he appeared, Rocky was a good guy, a man who was highly respected. Upon that silver screen he could do no wrong...make no mistakes...because there was always a director to tell him what to do, and a script that gave him just the right words to say. But we also know that Allan Lane was a fine actor and an action star who was in a class all his own. Allan

Beautifully-tooled boots (Rocky liked to wear spurs).

gave us so many hours of joy, pleasure and exciting adventures on Saturday afternoons, playing his role to perfection. For this we owe Allan "Rocky" Lane our thanks and our respect. What a legend he would have been if the studio had started making westerns with him in the very beginning.

Off the screen things were not the same. Allen had to do the best he could with whatever he had within him on any given day. He didn't always say the right things or do the right things, expected of him all the time. How many of us do! But you know something: that's life. There are no scripts for us to go by; you make up your own as you go on. Things do go wrong and you can't rewrite your mistakes in life as you can in a movie script. However, anyone who knows anything about the B-Western-Saturday-afternoon-cowboy-heroes, knows Allen "Rocky" Lane was a 6' 2", 190-pound, muscular, and handsome star who rode a jet-black horse. He was *the* good guy and a hero. We kids all idealized him so much, that each of us wanted to be another "Rocky" Lane.

I wonder how many more great western movies we would have seen of Rocky Lane, if the studios had seen the light and featured him as a western star, instead of miscasting

When Rocky rolled up his pant legs, so did thousand upon thousands of school kids.

him in those drawing room dramas and light comedies back in 1929. Allen might have been the top western star at Republic Studios or maybe even tops in Hollywood. Lane looked like a cowboy more than any of the other matinee cowboys — other than maybe Wild Bill Elliott and John Wayne!

Later he had a few supporting roles in TV shows like *Bonanza*, *Gunsmoke*, *Colt 45*, and *Cheyenne*. His best TV appearance was on the *Alfred Hitchcock Presents* in an episode entitled *"Lamb to the Slaughter."*

For all of you TV couch potatoes, the horse on the popular TV show *Mr. Ed*, well, he didn't really talk (you knew that). But did you know that the voice you heard was none other than that of Allan "Rocky" Lane. Lane never received any billing on the *Mr. Ed* series. It did give Lane a good income for a period of five years or so, allowing him to retire comfortably. Born in 1909, Lane passed away in 1973 at age sixty-four.

But in life...all good things have to come to an end...Allen Rocky Lane...there he goes down that...moonlit trail...but he'll return...soon again...no need to say good-bye...until then...so-long Rocky...so-long, till we meet again!

Thanks for the memories!

Rocky

For the exciting adventures in my happy days of youth.

Allan Young with Mr. Ed — whose voice was done from 1961-1966 by Lane.

THE ALL-AMERICAN COWBOY

JOHNNY MACK BROWN

JOHNNY MACK BROWN, "All American" football player at the University of Alabama — Johnny Mack Brown, "The All American Cowboy" and silver-screen hero was born on September 1, 1904. Johnny was born in Dothan, Alabama where he was one of nine children from one of the most respected old Alabamian families. His grandfather had been the first settler in the Dothan area.

Johnny's six-foot frame assisted his natural athletic abilities. He started playing football while in high school and in 1923 Brown enrolled at the University of Alabama. He tried out for the football team and easily made the grade.

 Johnny Mack Brown and one sidekick, Raymond Hatton.

In his first game against Georgia Tech, Johnny would catch one of the longest passes ever completed against that school. Holy Cow! In a game against the Kentucky Wildcats, Johnny ran a full 100 yards to score the winning touchdown. Johnny worked part-time in a local shoe store while attending college.

In 1924 Johnny Mack Brown was All Conference running back. At the start of the 1925 season Johnny was selected Captain of the team. In that year the team, lead by Johnny, went through their Southern conference schedule undefeated. Interestingly, another future screen cowboy, Charles Starrett, was on the Ivy League football team at Dartmouth College. Dartmouth received an invitation to play in the 1926 Rose Bowl but mysteriously turned it down. In its place, the University of Alabama was invited to the Bowl and they accepted the invitation.

On New Years Day in 1926 Johnny Mack Brown attained national fame for his reception of the longest touchdown pass to date in a Rose Bowl game. It went for sixty-five yards and Alabama to defeated the University of Washington 20 to 19.

Astride Rebel.

Johnny had explosive running power when he had the pigskin. In the third quarter of the Bowl game, with Washington leading 12 to 0, Johnny caught the afore-mentioned pass and scored a touchdown. He later caught a second touchdown pass. And he wasn't done yet! Johnny scored another touchdown on an end-around play that went for fifty-nine yards. He also knocked down a last second desperation pass by the UW team. This was truly a great day in Rose Bowl history and for young Johnny Mack Brown.

Johnny's college football career ended on a glorious note. For his outstanding play in the Rose Bowl he was named the MVP of the game. Previously he had been named All Southern Conference halfback for both the 1924 and the 1925 seasons. Johnny was famous for his pass catching and he was just as famous for his exciting end-around runs. The outstanding Alabama football team of 1925, coached by Wallace Wade, went undefeated.

In 1957, Johnny Mack Brown was inducted into the National Football Foundation Hall of Fame. He was the only Western film star who could make such a claim. At his induction ceremony he commented, "Because we were

the first team from the south to play in the Rose Bowl, we were supposed to be kind of lazy down South, full of hook-worms and all. Nevertheless, we came out here and beat one of the best teams in the country, making it a kind of historical event for Southern football. We didn't just play for the University of Alabama, we were playing for the whole South."

Paralleling the film careers of other former pigskin heroes such as John Wayne and Charles Starrett, Johnny Mack Brown found his transition into motion pictures as an actor rather easy. His first picture at MGM had a baseball theme, and starred William Haines. It was entitled *Slide Kelly Slide* and released in1927. Ten years later Johnny would be at the Rose Bowl to welcome his Crimson Tide when they played again in Pasadena.

Johnny's personal life wasn't put on hold while he awaited his entrance into the movies. Johnny married his college sweetheart, Cornelia "Connie" Foster, after the big Rose Bowl victory in 1926. She was the daughter of a prominent Tuscaloosa Judge. Over the years their marriage produced four children: Jane, John Lachlan, Cynthia, and Sally. By the age of twenty-three Johnny was just beginning his family — not to mention his movie career — both of which were to be long lasting.

Still displaying the build of a star football player at the University of Alabama.

After his first picture at MGM, Johnny moved up and into major films, co-starring with names like Greta Garbo, Marion Davies, Madge Bellamy, and Joan Crawford. Johnny had made eighteen pictures during his first three years in Hollywood. And soon he would make his first western film — an omen of things to come. In 1929 Warner Baxter earned an Oscar for best actor, in the picture **In Old Arizona** (a Fox film). In that same year, **The Virginian** starring Gary Cooper, was a top money producer.

As a result of the success of these films, MGM decided to enter the lucrative outdoor film market. For its first entry, it made a picture called **Billy the Kid** (1930) — the story of the famous young outlaw gunman of the old Southwest. Johnny Mack Brown played the famous outlaw gunfighter and Wallace Beery played his close friend and famous sheriff Pat Garrett. The film was shot on location in Lincoln County, New Mexico, where Billy the Kid had lived and died. In the film, Billy the Kid's own guns, which were borrowed from silent-screen cowboy William S. Hart, were worn by Brown.

Johnny worked again with Wallace Beery in a gangster movie titled **The Secret Six** (1931), and was joined by a

 Definitely the king of the well-blocked hat.

young MGM hopeful named Clark Gable. The studio was developing its young actors for bigger things and Johnny was put in competition with Gable for stardom. One of the drawbacks that limited his potential for particular roles was Brown's southern drawl. He did get good reviews for his performances, yet it was Gable that MGM decided to promote into their top star. When Johnny's contract ran out, MGM did not pick up his option.

Over the next few years Johnny moved from studio to studio, appearing in lesser films. He was no longer a rising young star. Brown's career was definitely at a low point. The great depression affected Hollywood film production and work was hard to find for many actors, extras, and stagehands. Johnny took roles at Poverty Row Studios just to have work.

As early as 1930 Johnny Mack Brown had shown that he could perform well in westerns. During these hard times it was a natural move for him to sign onto a series of B-Westerns. In 1935 Johnny hooked up with the newly-formed Supreme Pictures Studio, headed up by A.W. Hackel (the latter half of his films were distributed through Republic Studios). Bob Steele was already making westerns for Supreme when Brown arrived.

Johnny along with another sidekick, Fuzzy Knight.

1026-5

Eventually, Johnny Mack Brown became its other western star.

In 1933, before Johnny began his B-Western series with Supreme. He starred in his first serial, *Fighting With Kit Carson* (Mascot), which had been his first B-Western role and predated his B-Western features by more than a full year. Johnny portrayed the rugged frontiersman.

Johnny Mack Brown's first western picture for Supreme Studios was titled *Branded A Coward* and was not that good mainly because of the weak development of an interesting story. But his next picture was a dandy — maybe one of his best films overall. It was titled *Between Men* (1935). It tells the story of a son in search of his father who had been forced to flee as an outlaw years before. The father, played by William Farnum, believed his son had been killed in the incident that turned him into an outlaw. Robert N. Bradbury wrote the script and some people believed it might actually have been intended for his actor son, Bob Steele.

The Supreme films and those released by Republic were fine examples of B-Westerns. In addition to Hackel's production values, they sported such directors as Robert N.

Bob Baker (left) and Fuzzy Knight (center) join Johnny in a staged gun fight publicity shot.

Bradbury (Bob Steele's father), Sam Newfield, S. Roy Luby and Albert Ray. Johnny's leading ladies included Lois January and the beautiful Iris Meredith among others. The supporting casts sounded like a roll call of B-Western character actors, with the likes of William Farnum, George "Gabby" Hayes, Charles King, Jack Rockwell, Ed Cassidy, Dick Curtis, Bud Osborne, Frank LaRue and Al St. John. Villains, old codgers, sheriffs, henchmen, and ranchers — they were all there in Johnny's Supreme western pictures.

The Hackel-Republic Johnny Mack Brown series had firmly established Johnny as a B-Western star of the first order. The films were considered above average in story line, were extremely well acted and very well produced. Johnny Mack Brown was now headed for the top of the line in westerns at Universal Studios.

In 1935 Johnny moved to the larger production facilities at Universal for his second B-Western Serial, *The Rustlers of Red Dog*. This was another epic frontier story in which Johnny helps protect the settlers from Indians and renegade whites. Johnny was a peace officer, and his pals, Laramie, an old frontiersman played by Raymond Hatton, and Deacon, a gambler of sorts, played by Walter

Miller. Brown's next western serial offering was titled *Wild West Days* (Universal, 1937). In this one Johnny played a character called Kentucky — a frontiersman who goes to the aid of a brother and sister saves their mine.

By now Johnny's black garb had became his standard serial outfit and further established his western film persona. *The Oregon Trail* (Universal, 1939) was to be Johnny's final western serial. This epic featured Johnny as a frontier scout whose job it was to stop the raids on the wagon trains crossing the plains on their way to Oregon. Johnny's sidekick in this one was "Deadwood" played by no other than Fuzzy Knight. The old number one black-hat villain in western films, Roy Barcroft, fooled viewers by playing a good guy "Colonel Custer."

Johnny's first feature release for Universal was *Desperate Trails* which co-starred resident studio singing cowboy, Bob Baker, who was on his way out as a western star at this time. Johnny Mack Brown was brought to the film series to provide more believable action than the singing cowboy was able to do.

Johnny continued with Universal Studios until 1943 when he made his last duo western there with Tex Ritter in *The*

Lone Star Trail. Johnny Mack Brown went on to star in many more westerns at Monogram Studios. And Jimmy Ellison (Johnny from the Hopalong Cassidy series) would co-star in several of Johnny's films. In 1952 Johnny Mack Brown made his last B-Western film entitled **Canyon Ambush**.

With **Canyon Ambush** another western hero would soon ride off into the sunset. But Johnny Mack Brown would leave his mark on Hollywood. Johnny was second only to Charles Starrett (a.k.a. The Durango Kid) in the number of B-Western films actually made. Johnny Mack Brown made one hundred-and-eleven B-Westerns. At the end of his pictures he would often mount Rebel and ride off down the trail, that is, if he didn't get the girl.

Johnny died in November 1974 at the age of seventy, of kidney failure. Johnny had said before he passed away: "Don't feel sorry for me after I'm gone. I've had a full life and I've done about everything a man could ever want to do!"

But in life...All good things have to come to an end...Johnny Mack Brown...there he goes...down the moonlit trail...but he'll return...soon again...no need to

Beginning to show his age, but still able to hold his own against the bad guys.

say goodbye…until then…So-long Johnny Mack Brown …So-long till we meet again.

Thanks for the Memories,

Johnny

For The Exciting Adventures In My Happy Days of Youth

 Dashing studio publicity shot in front of drop screen.

CHAPTER 4

AMERICA'S FAVORITE SINGING COWBOY

GENE AUTRY

Whoopee Ti Yi Yo , Rockin'To And Fro
Put Him Back In The Saddle Again.
Whoopee Ti Yi Ya, Let Him Go On His Way,
Back In The Saddle Again.

I'm Back In The Saddle Again
Out Where A Friend Is A Friend
Where The Longhorn Cattle Feed,
On The Lowly Ginseng Weed.
I'm Back In The Saddle Again
Ridin'The Range Once More

BACK IN THE SADDLE AGAIN

Toting My Old forty-four,
Where Yea Sleep Out Every-night
And The Only Law Is Right.
Back In The Saddle Again.

Whoopee Ti Yi Yo, Rockin'To And Fro,
Back In The Saddle Again.
Whoopee Ti Yi Ya, I Go On My Way,
Back In The Saddle Again.

Whether he was training a horse, writing songs, or thrilling a motion picture audience, Gene Autry was always the happiest when he was "Back in the Saddle." Gene Autry was a bright shinning star of the cinematic old west and surely America's all-time favorite singing cowboy.

Every Saturday, if I could scrap up a dime, I would be right down town at the State Theatre (the best of the two theatres we had in town) just like everyone else that could! We all came to see this handsome cowboy on a big beautiful stallion, named Champion — going about, doing good. He could ride that horse, play a guitar, and sing a song all at the same time — while I was riding right there

Gene making use of a whip (not a lasso).

along beside him (on that broom-stick-pony of mine). And you know, his gun never ran out of bullets — especially when the bad guys had to be stopped. Some how his bullets never drew any blood, but the bad guys dropped nevertheless.

Before too long into Gene Autry's career, parents quit dropping the kids off at the theatre. Instead, they started coming to see the movie with them. What a wonderful sight it was to see after the movie: some of the parents would be carrying a child that had fallen asleep during the movie. That was something that I experienced while working at that theatre as a young man and have never seen since — and probably never will again. The love a parent had for his children and the love a child had for his or her parents — you just don't see it today as we saw it back in the days of the western heroes like Gene Autry, Roy Rogers and Hopalong Cassidy. These were real American heroes who were concerned about the image they presented to our young kids.

Gene Autry was the image of justice, goodness, and purity. And in the eyes of this poor little country boy, he made the world look better.

Non-publicity shot taken in Hollywood hills.

At the time Gene was born in 1907, on a farm near Tioga, Texas, the real west was still a living part of his reality. His great-grandparents traveled west in covered wagons and one of his relatives actually died at the Alamo. During his boyhood, Gene actually witnessed the end of the old West. He was raised in frontier towns in the old Oklahoma territory where the last of the great bank robbers — like the Dalton Gang — could still meet frontier justice.

As the real West faded, early moviemakers rushed to capture it on film. Gene's generation was the first to see the real West as it appeared in movies. Thomas Edison recorded Buffalo Bill's Wild West Show on film. The Miller Brothers 101 (pronounced "one-o-one") Wild West Show was acquired just to create a movie stock company — one that used real cowboys to chase real Indians across movie theatre screens. Gene could watch a real bank robber in action, right in his hometown. An Oklahoma outlaw, Al Jennings, was captured and did time. Jennings gave up his life of crime for an acting career and played himself in films. Shot in on location in Oklahoma, Jennings' kind of pictures showed the kind of poverty Gene would have seen as a child. The places and the people he saw everyday would prepare Gene for his destiny as a cowboy hero.

 There were a number of "Champions" that Autry rode over the years.

The first time a story was told on film in America, it was a western: a classic tale of bad guys holding up trains. ***The Great Train Robbery*** could have been a page right out of Gene Autry's life. At age seventeen, Gene got a job on the "Frisco Lines" and one night got a taste of the real West, when at gun point, he was robbed of the receipts from ticket sales. After handing over the money, Autry was locked up in one of the refrigeration cars while the outlaws made their getaway. This experience was like those dime novels that he read at the local barbershop — about Wild Bill Hickok and The James Boys.

At age ten, Gene took a job at the local movie house where he helped clean the theatre and deliver handbills around the community. Here Gene got his first look at cowboy heroes on the movie screen. As Gene admired Harry Carey and Tom Mix (and his "Wonder Horse" Tony), he had a good look at the type of cowboy hero he would later grow up to become.

The Autry family led a rural western life that prepared Gene for his later work in the saddle. Gene's father was a horse trader and would buy, sell or trade horses anytime of day or night. Gene's grandfather was a Baptist minister and his mother was a singer in the church chorus where Gene started singing at about five or six years old. Gene

Compare the white stripe on this "Champion" to the one on page 113.

GA-9

was nearly twelve years old when he bought his first guitar from a Sears catalog. From that point on it would be music that would lead Gene out of town. When a traveling medicine show came to town one summer, Gene got a job singing to warm up the crowd. He had learned at a young age how to sell a song, and he put that talent to use working the local cafes for pocket change.

Gene was a practical young man. He trained to be a telegraph operator, and was making good money working the graveyard shift, when a chance meeting with a stranger changed his life forever. The stranger came to the office to send a telegram, noticed Gene's guitar, and ask him to play a tune. The stranger — the famous humorist Will Rogers — liked his playing and singing and encouraged Gene to try to get radio audition. He encouraged him not to give up until he made it. Gene did as Rogers had instructed and not-to-long thereafter recorded his first big hit *Silver Haired Daddy Of Mine*. It sold a over a million copies and was the first record to be gold plated. That was the beginning of a tradition that has remained an important part of the recording industry to this very day.

Known on local radio stations as the "Oklahoma Yodeling Cowboy," Gene recorded more hit songs like *Comin'*

 *Gene made many a song a hit: from **Back in the Saddle Again** to **Rudolph the Red-Nosed Reindeer**.*

Around The Mountain. With his records selling through the Sears catalog, Gene was invited to Chicago to sing on the radio. Shortly afterward, Autry became a regular on the very popular *National Barn Dance* where he got to work with the first "million-seller cowgirl singer," Patsy Montana.

The radio years in Chicago proved to be the time for building life-long partnerships. Gene was out on the road when his accordion player got the flu. So Gene called a local young man named Smiley Burnette, who could play every instrument in the book. Smiley became his singing sidekick on radio and later in sixty motion pictures. Gene also formed another lifetime partnership during his radio days. Ina Mae Spivey was a college girl studying to be a teacher. During a quick visit to see her aunt and uncle in Chicago, Gene realized he had met the one for him. Ina would become an active part of Gene's career. Their spur-of-the-moment marriage would last for forty-eight happy years.

Sound had come to the movie westerns by 1930. A cowboy like Ken Maynard, who was famous for his trick riding and roping, would set your teeth on edge, however, when he tried to sing. Looking for new talent, Mascot

Gene and Smiley Burnette

Pictures decided to try out a radio star. This would be Gene's fateful Hollywood call.

After his successful audition for **In Old Santa Fe**, Gene was offered his first starring role and retained his name for his cowboy character. **The Phantom Empire** was the first and only western science fiction serial and it put Gene on the map as a singing cowboy star. The success of **The Phantom Empire** got Gene his first starring role in a feature films. It was **Tumbling Tumbleweeds** at Republic Studios. Shot in six days at a cost of $18,000, Tumbling Tumbleweeds was a hit. Republic Studios would be home for Gene for the next twelve years and fifty-eight western movies.

Republic Studios was forced to come up with a different format for a new kind of cowboy hero. Action, Singing, and Comedy would be trademarks of a Gene-Autry-western. Tom Mix had the greatest influence on Gene: he retained a Tom-Mix-style of action in his films but added his own unique character. If anyone ever had that clean-cut, All-American-Hero-type look, it was Gene Autry.

Gene Autry's movies could teach a kid the hard lessons of life but if Gene didn't get his hands on a bad guy soon

 Just one of his beautiful supporting actresses.

there would be a mad rush to the concession stand. The kids paid their hard earned dimes to see action. Gene could do running mounts, stagecoach transfers, and many more of his own stunts. Action in a Gene Autry picture always meant a big finish, it could be as simple as the good guy chasing the bad or as big as a landscape full of extras, in either case they would need lots of room to run and Lone Pine, California was the perfect location. Many of the Roy Rogers, Gene Autry and Hopalong Cassidy movies were shot there.

For many of Gene's fans the best parts of his movies was the romance, for others it was the action, but for many it was the singing, and for a great number of us it was the comedy and Smiley Burnette was the head of that department. Smiley Burnette was the first sidekick to enter the Motion Picture Heralds poll of the top ten western box-office stars, in fourth place in 1942 behind Gene Autry, Roy Rogers, and Hopalong Cassidy. Smiley also wrote scores of songs which he and Gene would record and sing in the Autry pictures. In 1940 Gene hit the radio with the "Melody Ranch" — his own weekly radio show and the show would stay on the air for sixteen years. Gene co-wrote **Be Honest With Me,** winning an Oscar nomination at the 1942 Academy Awards. Gene would co-write over

Cass County Boys

two hundred songs, record over six hundred and would sell over 50 million records.

With the war approaching Gene used song to tell his fans to do the right thing, by buying U.S. savings bonds. When the head of Republic Studios told Gene he would get him deferred from the service, his top box-office cowboy had something else in mind. Gene wanted to serve his country, so he enlisted and served as a transport pilot in the Pacific. While on a bond drive for the service in Texas, he ran onto some old musical friends — The Cass County Boys, and Gene promised to call them out to Hollywood as soon as the war was over. In November of 1945 they got a wire from Gene and joined him for Thanksgiving dinner at his California ranch. Gene had kept his word to the Cass County Boys.

While Gene was away during the war, some things had changed. Smiley was no longer under contract to Republic and had signed with another studio. After a contract dispute with Republic, Autry formed his own production company. In 1947 he released his first picture through Columbia Pictures: *The Last Round Up*. His new deal with Columbia Pictures gave him fifty percent of the profits. Gene Autry was never afraid to try something new always kept up with the style and challenges of the times.

Gail Davis (TV's Annie Oakley) and Pat Buttram, one of Gene's sidekicks

Gene needed a new sidekick, since Smiley was no longer available, so he picked up Pat Buttram who had been his sidekick on his radio shows. They would play together on tours, in movies, and on TV show for years to come.

A personal touch was always a part of Gene Autry's success, so he took his show on the road, letting his fans see their favorite singing cowboy in person. Gene built a strong relationship with young kids in such a way as to make fans out of whole families. Playing one-niters in small towns and big cities, Gene would set attendance records everywhere he appeared. Whether it was London, New York, or Boston, or all the towns in between, it was always the same: the entire town would turn out to see Gene Autry. Gene and his crew were the first group to play Madison Square Gardens after the war. And they packed the house for every show for one full month.

When the Gene Autry Show came to town, Gene would set aside time for the kids that couldn't make it to the show. In every town he went stopped, Gene would visit the kids in the hospitals and orphanages. That same crush of the crowds followed Gene Autry across oceans. Something genuine and something personal drew astounding crowds into the streets to see the singing cow-

Montage with Smiley Burnette on his horse Ringeye.

boy from another country—from another world. Once in Dublin, Ireland the crowd grew to an estimated crowd of 750,000 people. They flooded the streets to get a look at the world famous movie hero.

By 1940 Gene Autry had become the most popular western star in motion picture history. This little boy from Tioga, Texas who started out on a farm, who toiled in the cotton fields, working before he was in his teens, living through poverty during the Depression, and who served in World War II—this truly was an American hero. Gene Autry was America; he was good people—good folk. If, as a young person growing up, you wanted a hero to emulate, you would never have found a better example than Gene Autry. Gene did more to keep western American history alive and preserve our western heritage than any other person in Hollywood. He fulfilled a lifelong dream with his Gene Autry Western Heritage Museum located in Los Angles. Located on thirteen acres in Griffith Park with 140,000 square feet of interior space, the museum offered two special galleries for changing exhibitions and seven theme galleries with traditional museum settings – many designed to be interactive. Film, recordings, video, and special effects are used throughout. The museum features a permanent hands-on gallery for children. There is

also a 215-seat theatre, a library, an educational center, cafe, and a museum store.

The primary focus of the museum's collection is artifacts that relate to the real, everyday lives and occupations of the people who helped settle the west. As to the real west, the museum also depicts the west of romance and imagination as created by artists, authors, filmmakers. This is the area of the museum where you'll find exhibits on Gene Autry and other cowboy movie stars.

Gene Autry had a tremendous recording career that started in the late twenties and lasted until the early sixties. Gene met and became good friends with Johnny Marvin who had had some success in New York as a recording artist on the Victory label. Johnny Marvin became associated with Gene in business matters and cut back on his performing career. During World War II Johnny went out on tour to entertain the troops. While performing in the South Pacific, he became ill with a tropical sickness and died.

Another person who had a strong influence on Gene in the early years was Jimmy Long. Starting out together as telegraph dispatchers in Oklahoma, they discovered a

common love for composing songs. Together they wrote *That Silver-Haired Daddy of Mine* and it became one of Gene's biggest hits. Jimmy also sang with Gene on the recording of this hit as well as other early recordings. Ina Mae Spivey, Gene's first wife was Jimmy Long's niece. Without question, Gene Autry influenced several generations of country and western singers, but the one person that greatly influenced Gene as he struggled to establish his career was the singer-composer Jimmie Rodgers.

From 1927 to 1933 Jimmie Rodgers a railroad man, singer, composer, and recording artist became a country music legend. During these six brief years he laid the foundation for commercial country music, while selling some twenty million records. Rodgers composed many of Gene's early songs. Upon Jimmie's death in 1933, Gene recorded *The Life of Jimmie Rodgers* and *The Death of Jimmie Rodgers* in tribute to this country artist who had meant so much to him.

Gene's most frequent collaborator on song compositions was Fred Rose. Gene often commented that he recorded more than three hundred songs and helped write a third of them, mostly with Fred Rose. Fred Rose was from Nashville and is credited with discovering Hank Williams

*Ken Maynard was the star of **In Old Santa Fe** — the film that gave Autry his first exposure*

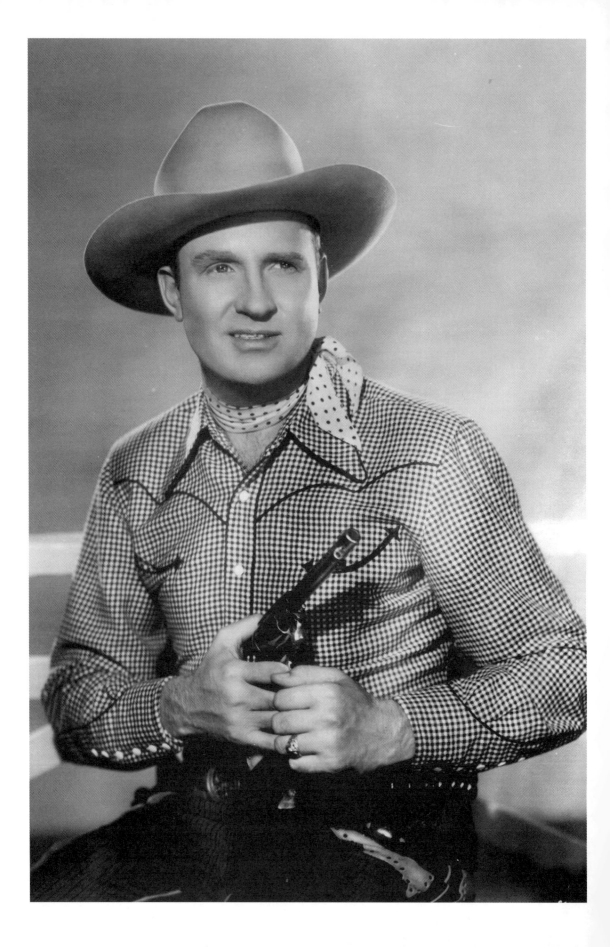

(the singer not the author). Fred and Gene worked well together and often would knock out songs overnight or sometimes in only a couple of hours when they were needed quickly for a particular scene in one of Autry's movies.

Gene Autry made his film debut as a dude ranch cowboy singer in a 1934 Ken Maynard film titled *In Old Santa Fe*. He quickly followed that performance by playing a bit role in a Ken Maynard serial called *Mystery Mountain* in 1934. By this time *In Old Santa Fe* had been released and the public reaction to the youthful cowboy singer was extremely positive. This, of course, did not go unnoticed by the officials at Mascot Studios who had made the film.

About this time Ken Maynard was due to star in another serial for the studio. This one was to be called *The Phantom Empire*. Suddenly Ken Maynard went on one of his frequent rampages with Mascot, a company that had grown weary of its temperamental western star. Nat Levine, the head of Mascot, decided to fire Maynard and take a chance on the young, inexperienced cowboy singer Gene Autry who had screen-tested so well for *In Old Santa Fe*. The rest, of course, cinematic is history.

202

From 1935 until 1953 Gene Autry starred in a total of ninety motion pictures. He quickly rose to the top of the B-western field and remained in first or second place among cowboy stars in terms of box-office draw throughout his long film career.

I never try to intentionally compare one western cowboy to another. To me, each one had a unique and special characteristic that made him slightly different from all the rest. For instance you can't compare a Autry film with a Hopalong Cassidy western because they are basically two completely different types of western films. Hopalong Cassidy was my hero and my favorite western cowboy, but you know, I loved this guy Gene Autry because to me he was truly All-American inside and out. Gene Autry became one of the world's most popular screen cowboys. He wore cowboy clothes all the time. In fact, his wife once said, "He even comes down to breakfast fully dressed in a cowboy suit, with tie and boots." He always wore Texas-made leather boots and had as many as fifty pair at a time. He said the only other pair of shoes he owned was his pair of golf shoes.

Gene Autry was, in my opinion and without doubt, the world's most versatile entertainer. After all, can you think

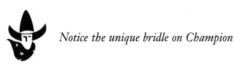

Notice the unique bridle on Champion

of any other star that was on top for so long in the movies, on radio, television, records, rodeos, or in stage shows? Gene was a goodwill ambassador wherever he went — whether in a foreign country or in the smallest or largest city in the United States.

Gene was a man who worked his way to the top the hard way and was a man to whom America and his faithful fans can always be proud. Public recognition for Gene's outstanding work over the years in the area of personal appearance shows came late. It wasn't until April of 1987, that the Hollywood Chamber of Commerce honored him with a fifth star on the Hollywood Walk of Fame. His previous stars were each for his work in films, radio, television, and records.

Gene Autry said at the ceremony, "Well, it means a lot to me. After all, a five-star general is as far as you can go." Gene is the only star to have received five stars on the Walk of Fame. Yes, Gene that's as far as you can go, and you went as far as a man could go in the entertainment field—doing it with class and style. The Autry magic kept rolling along until Gene past away in 1998. After starring in ninety feature films and ninety-one television episodes, unlike many of the B-western cowboy stars, the name of

Gene Autry became a legend. This is one cowboy that didn't ride off into the sunset forgotten after his western-cowboy-career days were over.

This cowboy carved his name forever into our American history.

But in life, all good things have to come to an end...Gene Autry...Gene...Autry...there he goes...down the moonlit trail...but he'll return...soon again...no need to say good-bye...until then...so-long...Gene...so-long...till we meet again.

Thanks for the Memories,

Gene

For The Exciting Adventures In My Happy Days of Youth

KING OF THE COWBOYS

ROY ROGERS

ROY ROGERS, WHO WAS BORN Leonard Slye in Duck Run (near Cincinnati), Ohio, was known and billed as the "King of the Cowboys." Roy was one of the most popular entertainers of all time in any media. Riding his famous palomino, Trigger, and most of the time seen with his favorite leading lady and wife, Dale Evans, Rogers rode across the silver screen to the enjoyment of movie goers young and old, parents and kids alike. He made eighty-two films for Republic Studios, during a career that spanned fourteen years and later had his own television series which was comprised of one hundred-and-one episodes. Rogers received star billing in two motion pictures that came after his own career — ***Son Of Paleface***,

Roy Rogers and Andy Devine

staring Bob Hope in 1952 and in *Mackintosh and T.J* in 1976.

Members of the Roy Rogers Fan Club bought 28 million *Roy Rogers* comic books each year, and prompted publishers to produce nineteen hardback-books based on his fictional heroics. They listened to him sing and yodel on old RCA Victor 78's. A true Roy Roger fan would say, "I was raised on Quaker Oats," and would stood ready to argue that their hero could ride, shoot, fight, and sing better than any other silver-screen cowboy. He probably could out sing my hero Hopalong Cassidy, but I don't know about, shooting and fighting. That right hand of Hoppy's…well, it kicked like a mule, and it surely would have KO'd Rogers every time.

This was a period in our lives when heroes were in bountiful supply. There were the likes of Roy Rogers, "King of the Cowboys," Gene Autry, "America's Favorite Singing Cowboy," and "The Most Famous Hero of the West," Hopalong Cassidy. Hoppy, Roy and Gene were three of the best ever to ride across that silver screen at the State Theatre back home in Kentucky. Maybe, just maybe, some, of the old town folk will restore the old theater. It is such a part of the town's history. Just maybe a few of the

What a handsome face. That checkered shirt became a hallmark.

people there will spend a few of those greenbacks that they think they are going to take with them to who-knows-where to restore a piece of this town's history.

You know, in time I even came to see what Roy saw in Dale Evans. Not only was she good looking, she was smart and she could ride a horse with the best of them. Her voice had that "Texas ring" in it. It was a nice voice when it came time to belt out a good old western song with Roy.

Dale Evans was born Francis Octavia Smith on October 31,1912 in the home of her grandparents in Uvalde, Texas. At one time she took a job at radio station WHAS in Louisville, Kentucky as a female vocalist. The program director at the Louisville station gave her two things upon her arrival: a well-paying job (something she had never had before) and a new name. The new name: Dale Evans —which as we all know, she still carries to this day. The name suited her. In fact, she was thrilled over the idea of having a stage name. To Dale it signified that meant she was heading in the right direction.

In the good old days, when we had the trinity — Roy Rogers, Gene Autry and Hopalong Cassidy, you would see the young kids playing and identifying themselves

Mrs. Rogers (Dale Evans) joined by Gabby Hayes

with those characters. Today the young kids don't have anyone of that caliber with which to identify. Now, if you want to talk about realism, in today's movies, they'll beat a man up, kick him down two flights of stairs, break a board over his head and stab him a couple of times before shooting him three or four times — and he'll still be fighting. Now come on. Is that what you call realism? Just how much punishment do you think a human body can really take!

Leonard Franklin Slye (Roy to you and me) was born on November 5, 1911. His parents, like many others in Ohio at the time, were common working-class people. And of course, Roy was expecting to follow in the same footsteps when he grew up. He did start out the same way as most others in Ohio by taking a job in a shoe factory. It appeared as if he would make a career out of that job. He had all the makings of a factory worker and he didn't seem to have any other goals or dreams. The only thing that may have been different about him was his love for music. He loved to sing along with the songs that he heard on the radio, and even bought a guitar to accompany himself. But Roy didn't have any expectations that his singing would ever become anything more than it was: a vehicle for personal joy and relaxation. It was a good thing that he did

More "Roy Rogers" than Leonard Slye.

care for music, because it was that love for it that was going to change his whole life.

Actually, it was his love for his sister that started the ball rolling. At 17, Roy drove out to California to see his sister and ended up staying there for about three months. Upon his return to Ohio, he started to miss California so much that he hitchhiked back and there he stayed. Even in California he didn't yet have any desire to do anything special. Roy took any job he could get. He drove a truck, and picked peaches.

One day Roy and his cousin Stanley Slye put an act together and played the Hippodrome in downtown Los Angles. That did it, now Roy had a dream: he wanted to be in show business. One Saturday he and Stanley appeared on an amateur show called *Midnight Frolic*. Their act consisted of singing and yodeling. Two days later Roy joined a singing group called the Rocky Mountaineers. And within the next two years Roy had organized the Sons of the Pioneers.

Roy Rogers was an incredible success story if ever there was one. Here you had a poor unknown farm boy, from an equally unknown region of the country, making it big as a

Roy is joined by the Sons of the Pioneers.

singing cowboy-movie star — all resulting from a series of fortunate events.

Here's one great example: Roy went into a small shop in Glendale, California one day to have his hat cleaned (something you don't hear of any more). While he was waiting a guy comes in, all excited, saying he had to have his cowboy hat back immediately. Republic Pictures, he claimed, was looking for a new singing cowboy and he had to get out to the studio that afternoon. Roy, hearing the story, packed up his old guitar and drove out there as well. When Roy got there he wasn't able to get through security at the main gate. Even though he had worked in a couple of Gene Autry movies, he still didn't have any good studio contacts. So Roy waited around, and when he saw the extras coming back from lunch break, he just joined the group and walked right through the gate with them. Roy hadn't walked far when he felt a hand on his shoulder. Thinking that security had caught up with him, he was surprised to see an official of Republic (Sol Siegel) who had recognized him from a stint he had done with the Sons of the Pioneers. He asked Roy if he was there to test for the new singing cowboy role and Roy told him that was his intention, but he didn't know what to do or who to see. The friend told him that the studio had tested 17

guys already. When asked if he had brought his guitar along, Roy said, "Yes, I'll run out to the car and get it." But he told the fellow, "you be certain the security guard lets me back in, since I had to pull a little sneaky to get in here in the first place."

Roy auditioned as he planned and Republic selected him. When asked if anyone had him under contract, Roy had to tell them that he was with Columbia. At the time, he was working with the Sons of the Pioneers in some Charles Starrett films. Columbia agreed to release Roy if he would find someone to take his place. Roy, in turn, got Pat Brady. When Mr. Briskin listened to Pat, he was impressed enough to give Roy the "OK" — saying, "if that Republic deal works out for you okay, you're released."

At Republic Studios on October 13, 1937 Roy Rogers signed a contract for a whopping $75-a-week. Republic decided that the name "Len Slye" wouldn't work for a singing cowboy. Roy and several others met in the office of Mr. Yates (head of Republic) and they kicked around several names. Finally the name "Rogers" came up and Len said he liked it because he always did like Will Rogers. Next, someone mentioned "Roy" and the two names were put together. They sounded pretty good: Roy

How many faces can you identify in this casual gathering of matinee cowboys?

Rogers. And that's how the "King of the Cowboys" got his name. Once the name thing was settled Roy went down to the courthouse and went through the process required by law to have his name legally and permanently changed to Roy Rogers.

The publicity department repeatedly informed Roy he had to have what was called a "proper image." Roy Rogers, it was decided (by the PR department), was a true-blue son of the West, born in Cody, Wyoming, and raised on a cattle ranch. As the story went, he even was supposed to have labored as a ranch-hand in New Mexico for a while before making his way to Hollywood. It didn't take long for some of the publicity to back fire. Once a letter arrived from a unhappy group of citizens from Cody who were more concerned with historical accuracy than all the Hollywood hype. They claimed their research revealed absolutely no evidence of anyone named Roy Rogers having ever been born in the whole state of Cody — much less Wyoming.

You know the good Lord must have wanted Roy Rogers to be a cowboy. Look at the way things worked out for him. If he had not been in that hat shop on that specific day, at that specific time, and if he had been a few feet —

The man and his horse — Trigger was a beautiful palomino.

one way or the other — behind or ahead of Mr. Siegel of Republic Studios, the two men might never have met. If those things had not worked out the way they did, there may have never been a Roy Rogers, "King of the Cowboys."

One more event took an interesting twist for Roy. When the studio riding stables brought over some horses for Roy to try out, Trigger was about the third horse Roy tried-out. After that, he didn't ride another horse. He knew that there was no other horse he wanted to be seen riding. He thought Trigger was the prettiest horse he had ever seen.

After Roy's first film, he went to Clyde Hudkins, the owner of Trigger, and asked to buy the palomino. Roy told Mr. Hudkins that if he would sell Trigger to him, that he would do his best to influence the studio in to using Hudkins' horses in all of Roy's movies. That was an offer he couldn't walk away from and he agreed to sell Roy the horse for $2,500 — telling Roy that he could paid for the horse "a little at a time." That was a lot of money for a man only making $75 a week. Nevertheless, they shook hands and Trigger was Roy's.

Trigger was part thoroughbred and that is where he got his speed. It was Smiley Burnette who suggested to Roy that he name the horse "Trigger." The beautiful palomino would be with Roy throughout his movie career and live to the age of thirty-three.

Roy's first motion picture for Republic was ***Under Western Stars*** and was completely shot in Hollywood. The plot featured a so-called Wyoming cowboy who goes to Washington, and when it premiered in April of 1938 it did so at the Capital Theatre in — where else — Dallas, Texas. Figure that bit of logic out.

The studio hired the Sons of the Pioneers, to make the trip for the premiere and the put on a stage show before the showing of the film. Reporters turned out in force for interviews and pictures, and it was in the ***Dallas Morning News*** that Roy got his very first review. If he wasn't already hooked on the movie business, the review did the trick. The reviewer wrote: "The movie introduces young Mr. Rogers as a new cowboy hero, real out west and not the drugstore variety. This lad isn't the pretty-boy type, but a clean-cut youngster who looks as if he had grown up on the prairies, not backstage with a mail order cowboy

suit. An engaging smile, a good voice and an easy manner out to put him in front before too long."

For the next two years at Republic, the cost of handing his fan mail alone exceeded the salary the studio was paying him. Roy did one night stands at the movie theatres for $150 to help pay the cost for answering his fan mail — since Republic refused to help out with the expense.

When Leonard Slye went to work for Republic he took on the role of Roy Rogers. Later in contract negotiations, and in lieu of more money, he gained legal rights to the name *Roy Rogers* along with the legal rights to merchandise the name — which he had legally changed earlier. In a similar fashion, William Boyd, in lieu of additional money, negotiated and gained rights to *Hopalong Cassidy* and some of the *Hoppy* movies.

I guess Hoppy, Roy and Gene were the top three western stars of their day — an era in which western movies were the single, top attraction in our country. Maybe Hoppy, Roy and Gene, along with the other stars of the B-westerns, will never achieve the acclaim they deserve for their contributions to of the movie industry in general, not-to-mention our cultural history. But I'm sure that many who

 Smiley Burnette (cupcake pans stacked next to newsprint type?)

grew up in the 1940's — like a lot of us, didn't escape the powerful influence of Roy Rogers, Gene Autry, and Hopalong Cassidy.

The thundering success of **Under Western Stars** left little question of whether or not the familiar Republic eagle was going to keep flying so proudly — even if Gene Autry never came to terms with the studio. He did later of course, but the studio wasted little time in 1938 in getting four more Rogers' pictures into the movie houses. Roy's next starring role came in **Billy the Kid Returns**.

To add a touch of romance, Lynn Roberts was cast in the female lead and again Gene Autry's old sidekick, Smiley Burnette, provided the comedy. The success of Rogers and Hart musicals on Broadway prompted Mr. Yates to change Lynn Roberts' name; henceforth she would be known as Mary Hart—and his own version of Rogers and Hart would be billed as the **Sweethearts of the West**. That lasted for six pictures. However, in time Westerns began to wear on Miss Hart, and she decided to reclaim her own name and seek other avenues for he acting skills.

By 1939, Smiley Burnette was back playing the fall-guy to Gene Autry's hero role and a search was on for a new side-

George "Gabby" Hayes — one of the truly great supporting actors in Westerns.

kick for Rogers. The role, briefly filled by Raymond Hattan, eventually fell to George "Gabby" Hayes who had managed to get out of a contract which called for him to play the role of Windy Halliday, an old codger teamed with Bill Boyd in the highly popular *Hopalong Cassidy* series. Deep personal conflicts had developed between Hayes and Boyd, and once released, Hayes signed with Republic. He joined Smiley Burnette in a couple of Gene Autry movies before the studio teamed him with Roy. It would be the beginning of a fruitful professional relationship and, perhaps even more important, a long-standing friendship. The two would remain close friends long after their movie partnership ended. Until his death at age eighty-four, Hayes was a frequent houseguest of Roy and Dale. Gabby was like a father, a buddy and a brother to Roy. I think Roy realized what an exceptional actor Gabby really was, while most others did not.

Hays was born in Wellsville, N.Y. and was working in vaudeville while just a kid. He and his wife, a dancer, married when they were sixteen years old, and worked on stage together for years before he ever came out to Hollywood. The Gabby Hayes seen on the screen and the real man nothing alike. For instance, he was easily one of the best-dressed men in Hollywood. He would drive onto

Roy Rogers
+ Trigger

the Republic lot in his Lincoln convertible, dressed to kill. He would go into his dressing room, take out his teeth, and put on his old western clothes and hat and would emerge all stooped over. Suddenly he was George "Gabby" Hayes.

Once, upon returning from a trip Roy had a message to call Gabby ASAP. So Roy phoned him up and the first thing Gabby said was, "Roy, while you were gone there was almost a disaster. Dumb me, got it in my mind to shave my beard off, and after I did I almost died. I don't ever remember me being so ugly. So Roy, don't worry if you don't see me for a while. I'm not even going to stick my head out the door until the dang thing grows back and I look my pretty self again." Hayes was one of those actors who recognized the need for a particular identity, and he happily settled on "Gabby" Hayes. It paid off. It made Hayes a rich man before he called it a career.

There was one critic among all others who Gabby always listened to. Soon as one of a film came out he would take his wife to see it. The next day, depending on her judgment, he would come around all excited or down-in-the-dumps. "Maw really liked this one," he tell people, or "Maw didn't care much for this one." Gabby Hayes

167

Autographed photo.

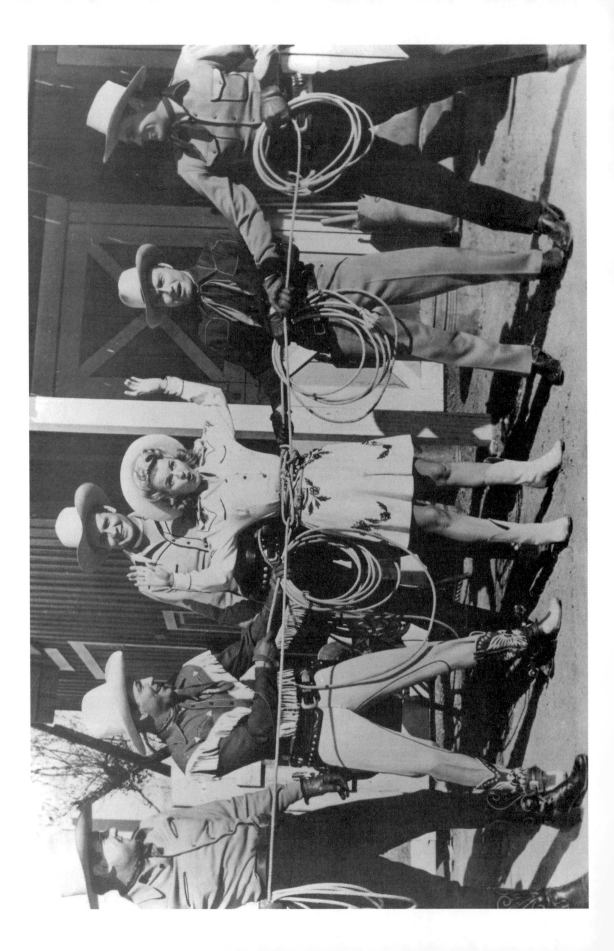

became a very lonely man in the years after his wife died. After her death, Gabby died a little too. He never again had that old enthusiasm for which he was known.

It didn't take too many personal appearances, promoting his movies, for Roy to recognize one of the basic requirements a movie cowboy was duty-bound to fulfill before he would be completely accepted. William S. Hart, the pioneer western star had set the precedent when his pinto Fritz became as popular with the audiences as he had. Hopalong Cassidy had Topper, Tom Mix had Tony, Gene Autry had Champion and Ken Maynard shared billing with his horse Tarzan. Soon it became Roy Rogers and Trigger — a cowboy-horse partnership that lasted until Trigger's death in 1965.

Trigger was his "stage name," but this palomino's registered name was Golden Cloud. He appeared in the *Adventures of Robin Hood* and was ridden by Olivia De Havilland. This was before being acquired by Roy Rogers.

One day Roy got in touch with Glenn Randall, a former rodeo performer who had a reputation as an expert horse trainer. Roy had a rodeo appearance in Baltimore scheduled in just over a month and he wanted Trigger to learn

Dale Evans is tied up by Roy and some friends. Can you identify Don "Red" Barry? Can you name the others?

a few simple tricks to use in the appearance. Unlike so many trainers, who rewarded horses with cubes of sugar after they had properly followed their cue, Glenn explained that a pat, a kind word or maybe an occasional carrot would get the trick done just as effectively. And with this method of training you would not have a beggar on your hands once the training was over.

Trigger wasn't the only one who was beginning to learn a few things. After Roy was well established as a western star, Herb Yates gave him a different type of script to study. Republic was planning to shoot a movie called **Front Page**, and Yates wanted Roy to play the part of a cocky newspaper reporter. Rogers didn't see any rhyme or reason to do this movie, especially since he was established as a western star. The result was a heated argument between Rogers and Yates. "In that case Roy," Herb said, "maybe we will just have to put some other cowboy on Trigger and let him do your next movie." Then Roy gave Yates a few heated words: "You may get someone else to do the next picture but he won't be riding Trigger because I own him." Once aware that Trigger did belong to Roy, Yates signed Lloyd Nolan for the part in **Front Page** and Rogers went on about his business being the singing cowboy.

Roy and Dale are joined by sidekick Pat Brady and Estelita Rodriguez.

Herb Yates never really gave up on the idea of Roy working in other type of films, and he and Roy would go through the same old argument time-and-time-again. Roy did do one of Yates' other projects in 1940 and it was a far cry from a B-Western. He ended up playing a hot-headed scalawag in **Dark Command**. Gabby Hayes, who also had a strong role in the movie, and it was he who actually persuaded Roy to do the picture. They were in pretty good company. The picture had a cast that included John Wayne, Walter Pidgeon, Claire Trevor, and Marjorie Main. Roy felt more comfortable in the saddle on Trigger and was soon back filming **Red River Valley** and **The Carson City Kid**—long before **Dark Command** premiered to good reviews and packed houses.

Trigger liked having Roy back in Westerns, too, especially since he was being billed as the "Smartest Horse in the Movies" and his unique talents were even being written into many of the scripts. Over the years Trigger received a couple hundred pieces of fan mail a week. He was also insured for $100,000.

After his first couple of years in Hollywood and tasting some success in the movie industry, Roy was still counting pennies, living in a small frame house, and wondering

Allen "Rocky" Lane and Monte Hale bookend Roy.

where the money he had heard movie stars were supposed to make. Roy tried to supplement his income by opening a western apparel store called "The Hitching Post" out in Studio City, but about all that venture proved was that as a businessman Roy Rogers made a pretty fair cowboy. By the end of 1939 Roy had made thirteen pictures, and was constantly worried about making it to the next paycheck. That's about the time Roy met Art Rush. And if Roy had known what Rush would be able to do for him in the years to come, he would probably have given Art a big hug instead of a skeptical handshake.

One day Roy got a call from Rush, who a specialist in talent management. He suggested it might be beneficial to both of them if they could meet for lunch. Art persisted, so Roy suggested they meet at Eaton's a Restaurant just across the street from Republic Studios. Art Rush was one of those people who arrived on the West Coast with his sleeves rolled wasting no time making a mark for himself. Art explained to Roy that he had grown tired of the corporate rat race and had decided to go into business for himself—maintaining a small group of performers that he represented. At the time they met he was managing Nelson Eddy, a star at MGM, and The Sportsman Quartet who appeared on Jack Benny's radio show. Art

Who's got who hogtied?

further explained that he needed a Western singer to complete his list. Roy thought "he needs me like he needs a whole in the head." Roy thought there was a pretty wide stretch of ground between a Nelson Eddy and a $150-a-week singing cowboy. Art was familiar with Roy's work and liked what he heard. His game plan was not to have any clients whose careers would be in direct conflict.

No one remotely did the kind of work Roy did and Rush had already heard that Rogers was looking for a manager. Roy explained he had already spoken with the William Morris Agency and felt a moral obligation to go with them. To Roy's surprise and relief, Art pressed the issue no farther. Instead, they spent the rest of lunch just chatting. Agent or no agent, Art was one of the most likable people Roy had come in contact with in the business. As Art and Roy got ready to leave Roy reached in his pocket for a tip and asked Art, "Where are you from?" "Ohio," Art replied. "I'm just a small town boy. Even had a pony and horse myself when I was a kid. I can ride." That did it. So much for William Morris and moral obligations. "Mr. Rush," Roy said, "we've got ourselves a deal."

That handshake over a table at Eaton's is the closest thing to a contract that Roy and Art ever had. It was that way for

The famous duo of Carl "Alfalfa" Switzer and "Spanky" McFarland from the **Our Gang** *and* **Little Rascals** *series.*

thirty-eight years. During that period of time Art was not just the only manager Roy ever had, but Roy's best friend as well. However…Roy never let Art forget that he wasn't altogether truthful that day they shook hands for the first time at Eaton's Restaurant. To Art's credit, he did grow up in Ohio, but Roy found out later Art was actually born in Pennsylvania.

Soon the work Roy was doing away from Republic was earning him more money than his acting job. It did escape Roy that his appearances in the movies were opening the doors on which Art Rush was so successfully knocking. Rush told Roy one day that he was in position he and Arlene could move out of that little frame house they lived in. Roy asked how much Art thought he could afford to spend. Roy was told somewhere in the $10,000 range. Those were the words Roy had been waiting to hear for a long time. He immediately went to look at a place he had in mind in the San Fernando Valley. He knew of a small chicken ranch, complete with 3,500 chickens and a comfortable white bungalow on the property. He told a puzzled Jim Osborne to close the deal as quickly as possible.

Once all the papers were signed, Roy picked up his parents, Andy and Mattie Slye, and drove them out to see the

place. As they all stood on the front porch, Roy handed his father the key to the front door. "Welcome home Dad," Roy said. "You're going to be getting all the sunshine you want now, tending to all those chickens." Inside the house Mattie found a large bolt of material and Roy told her "I thought you would want to make your own curtains."

Roy had never mentioned anything about it as far as Art Rush knew. But buying that home for his folks was something he had planned for a long time. He didn't do it with a lot of fanfare, but he did it with class. The place hadn't taken the entire $10,000, so Roy took the balance and filled dozens of sugar bowls with cash and put them in his mother's pantry where she would find them later.

Rush made sure no grass grew under Roy's feet. If Roy wasn't working on or promoting a picture or doing the radio show, Rush had him doing personal appearances somewhere around the country. In 1941, one of those trips took Roy to several large cities including Louisville, Kentucky. While entertaining at an orphanage, beautiful little girl about three-years-old hung onto Roy's neck throughout his entire visit. When Roy got ready to leave, she was still clinging to him, and as the nurse took her away she was crying, "Take me with you, take me with you!"

181

*Movie poster for **The Arizona Kid** (1939) in which he portrayed a character named "Roy."*

Roy never got over that scene, and on his way home from Louisville he stopped at Republic Pictures Exchange in Dallas, Texas, to ask Bob O'Donnell and Bill Underwood if they knew where he could adopt a child. They said, "you came to the right place." They were on the Board of Directors of Hope Cottage — a home for orphaned and abandoned children. At the time of Roy's visit, there were forty-two babies at the cottage. After going from bed to bed, Roy stopped at the fifth bed, where a pair of pretty brown eyes looked right up at him. He looked no further. A beautiful little girl with curly blonde hair and the prettiest brown eyes had captured his heart and Roy told them he wanted this baby. After checking Roy out and waiting till the baby was four-months-old, Cheryl Darlene became the Rogers' first child. But there would be more children — especially after Roy married Dale Evans.

In 1944 *Cowboy and the Senorita* was the first film to pair Roy up with heroine Dale Evans. Roy married Dale in 1947, making them a winning team on and off the silver screen.

One of the things Roy really missed since moving to California was having some good hunting dogs around. As far back as Roy could remember, there had always been plenty of dogs in his life —ready to spend the night chasing a fox or treeing a raccoon. And so, when he moved to his new home, he got in touch with some people he knew as avid hunters and started rounding up some dogs. It wasn't difficult with the number of strays coming around looking for a handout and would end up staying. The number grew to almost twenty before he knew it.

They would be far less trouble than the young man who was to become his number-one hunting partner. Outside of individuals directly associated with the motion picture business, you couldn't find many people who could tell you who Carl Switzer was. On the other hand, ask if those same people were familiar with Alfalfa, the gangly, freckle-faced kid in the **Our Gang** and **Little Rascals** comedies, and you would be hard pressed to find anyone who didn't know him. Fewer people even called him Carl. To everyone he was Alphie. When Roy met him he was about seventeen and his days as a child star were already behind him. But, he was still a rascal, lovable, friendly, and a great guy to have around —that is, when you weren't seriously considering wringing his neck.

For instance, there was the time he came to see Roy all excited about a bear hunt he had organized. A sizable group of hunters had, he explained, agreed to pay him a hundred dollars apiece if he would lead their expedition and furnish the hunting dogs. He told Roy, "I can make a killing on this deal if you'll loan me your dogs for the hunt." Not only did Roy agree to loan Alphie the dogs, but he suggested Alphie take his jeep. Some where along the way Alphie met a girl, fell madly in love (something he did with regularity), and found it necessary to sell not only Roy's jeep but also sold Roy's best lead dog to finance the romance. It was a while before Alphie came around after that. Eventually he did come around apologizing profusely, and Roy wound up telling Alphie things were "OK" — because Roy liked the kid and Switzer was his best hunting buddy.

Like so many highly successful child actors who were supposed to come into big bucks when they turned twenty-one, Alphie found out when the time finally came that the money was already gone. Alphie was never happy for any length of time — except when he and Roy were out hunting. That to him was the greatest thing in the world.

Roy and Alphie were good friends and hunting companions for fifteen years before he died in 1959, shot to death in an argument over $30 he thought some guy owed him for taking care of his dogs. $30! What a waste!

By this time in Roy's career he was financially secure, had a loving wife and two daughters who were the lights of his life. And then, as if the American Dream had no ending, Arlene gave birth to a son on October 28, 1946. News of the arrival of Roy, Jr., a healthy boy who would come to be known as Dusty, was spread throughout the world by the wire services. Six days after the birth of the baby, Roy had a Sunday morning golf date with Art Rush. Roy had been so excited about the arrival of his son that production of his current movie had been shut down for a week. A round of golf had been suggested, because it might be good for Roy and help him burn off his excess energy.

Before he left home to meet his golfing partner, the phone rang in his home. It was the hospital, urging him and Arlene's mother, to hurry to the hospital. When they reached Arlene's room they found it crowed with stern-faced doctors and nurses. Arlene was unconscious — the victim of a sudden embolism. Artificial respiration, injections, and oxygen had failed to do revive her. Shortly after Roy arrived, Arlene Rogers died.

It would be Mary Jo Rush who answered the phone some time later and rushed upstairs to wake her sleeping husband "I don't know who it is on the phone," she told her husband, "but it sounds urgent. It sounded like a child crying to me." Lifting the receiver, Art Rush heard the sobbing of Roy Rogers say the words that sent a frozen chill through his body: "Art, Arlene's dead." Suddenly Art was crying as well. "Where are you," Art asked. "Hospital" Roy responded. Art told Roy to stay where he was; "I'm on my way." Art got dressed, said a prayer, and headed to the hospital.

When Art got there he saw something that he would remain in his mind for the rest of his life. There was Roy standing next to his car in the parking lot, tears rolling down his checks and kids surrounding him. He was signing autographs—crying and signing autographs. Art later said: "I know the grief that he was bearing was far greater than mine, but that scene just broke my heart. There he was, his spirit broken, not even trying to hide his tears, but still signing the pieces of paper all those little kids were holding out to him."

But in life...all good things...have to come to an end ...Roy...Trigger...and Gabby...there they go...down the moonlit trail...but they will return...soon again...no need to say good-bye...until then...so-long Roy...so-long Trigger...so-long Gabby...until we meet again!

Thanks for the Memories,

Roy

For The Exciting Adventures In My Happy Days of Youth

Since the days of the Roy Rogers' movies, a whole different breed of people have emerged. The schools are different, The courts are different, the whole country is different. Today the word seems to be extreme. Unless producers go to extremes in a movie with sex, violence and language, people just don't seem to want to see it. Roy often said that he wouldn't let Trigger watch most of the stuff they play in movie theatres today.

CHAPTER 6

AMERICA'S MOST-BELOVED COWBOY

TEX RITTER

For ten years and sixty western movies, Tex Ritter blazed at the bad guys across the silver screen with a six-gun in each hand. He could handle fistfights more convincingly than any of the other singing cowboys. "Roy and Gene sang more—I killed and fought more—I must have killed old Charlie King at least twenty times," reminisced Tex. "Usually behind the same rock," he added. Tex galloped

across the screen on his beautiful white stallion White Flash — cameras shooting close-ups during a hard ride so that the audiences could see that Tex was not actually using a double.

More than any other sagebrush star, Tex Ritter preserved the music of the old West, singing old-time cowboy ballads with obvious enjoyment in his rich deep voice. It is still fun to watch old Tex Ritter films — Tex in his big white hat, two six-guns blazing, riding that striking white horse, brawling with Charlie King. But the best part of watching a Tex Ritter movie was to enjoy Tex's performing traditional Western music.

Tex Ritter arrived in Hollywood just as the singing cowboy became popular. Only Gene Autry and Roy Rogers, who starred in about ninety films each, made more musical westerns than Tex Ritter. If Ritter had worked for a major studio early in his career, his success might have equaled that of Autry or Rogers.

Instead, Tex starred for years with Grand National, Monogram and PRC — Poverty Row outfits that could not provide him with proper budgets, scripts or promotion. And years later when he did films for major studios,

 *Tex astride White Flash.*

Columbia and Universal, Tex was saddled with co-stars like Wild Bill Elliott and Johnny Mack Brown who were given the dominant roles.

Although Tex Ritter starred in poorly mounted films, and considering that he was mired in secondary co-star roles in more than a quarter of his movies, he still earned repeated recognition as one of Hollywood's most appealing western actors. If his movie career was not what it might have been, he nevertheless developed a legion of Tex Ritter fans that would loyally support him for three more decades. The little boy who rode his broom stick pony around his yard in Murvaul, Texas had become a two-gun, cowboy hero who rode a magnificent white stallion.

When Tex Ritter arrived in Hollywood in 1936 to star in B-Westerns, such films made up a large part of the motion picture industry's revenue. Major studios maintained B units to produce westerns, mysteries, and other short features, while a number of small independent studios concentrated their total efforts on B movies.

During the era of silent films, Bronco Billy Anderson, William S. Hart, Fred Thomson, hard-riding Ken

*The great villain Charles King who "was killed more times than any other bad guy in motion pictures" and got his start as a child in **Birth of a Nation** in 1915.*

Maynard, flamboyant Tom Mix, and a host of not-so-well-known cowboy heroes churned out western movies by the hundreds. The historic West of cattle drives, outlaws and gunfighters, had only recently passed into history and young audiences thrilled to the screen adventures of heroic cowboys sporting six-guns and big hats. The emphasis was on action: chases, fistfights, and shootouts. The western motion picture, with its sweeping scenery and galloping horses, was perfect for the big silver screen. Motion pictures needed movement, and the western movies "moved."

During the 1930's cowboy films were the most popular movies. Hollywood filmed about three hundred B-Westerns per year. For three decades these films had been produced by the hundreds, and as the formula began to grow stale. The musical tradition of the singing cowboy seemed to offer fresh possibilities. Early sound westerns, in the interest of economy, did not insert background music. The dialogue was simple, and many of the cowboy stars delivered their lines awkwardly. Fans loved the western for its action — not acting. The action seemed flat without the exciting musical strains once provided by silent movie theater pianists.

195

 Tex had a great smile and tremendous singing voice.

Ken Maynard tried short musical interludes in some of his films, as did young John Wayne. Wayne's singing voice had to be dubbed, and in one experiment, Wayne, as Singin' Sandy proved disastrous. Ken Maynard engaged Gene Autry, then a Chicago radio star, to deliver musical numbers in his movies.

After appearing twice with Ken Maynard in 1934, Gene Autry starred the following year in *The Phantom Empire*, a science fiction serial with a western setting. The role was intended for Maynard, but the studio replaced the cantankerous star with Gene Autry. Gene Autry was physically unimpressive and uncomfortable as an actor, but he was pleasant and sang well and audiences responded in large numbers to his films. Soon he sang his way through *Tumbling Tumbleweeds*, the first of a series of musical westerns that established Autry as a major box-office draw. Gene Autry was a screen phenomenon by 1935 and alert producers began to scout for other potential singing cowboys.

On most weekends Tex Ritter worked on a New Jersey dude ranch. Ed Finney of Grand National Pictures discovered him there. Tex signed a personal services contract with Finney, rather than with Grand National. The movie

Ken Maynard tried his hand at singing in his movies but gave it up in favor of using Gene Autry.

executive shrewdly reasoned that if Tex Ritter clicked as a star, then Ed Finney would direct and profit from Ritter's career.

Ed Finney, investing his own money in the Tex Ritter project, organized a production unit called Boots and Saddles to film the *Range Rider* series. The series was modestly budgeted at $8,000 to $12,000 per film. From this budget Tex would be paid $2,000 for each film. B-Westerns would be expected to earn at least $50,000, which provided solid profits with minimal investment for the studios. As producer, Ed Finney put together the Boots and Saddles unit, while assembling a cast and commissioning a script for the first Tex Ritter western film, *Song of the Gringo*.

Finney also put together an experienced cast to support his inexperienced star. Dark haired, leading lady Joan Woodbury had already played opposite William Boyd (Hopalong Cassidy) and Tim McCoy Playing Tex's first sidekick was Fuzzy Knight. The sheriff was played by Monte Blue and the bad guys were Warner Richmond and the towering Glenn Strange — who had been a heavyweight boxer and a stuntman and who later would earn

Surprisingly, even John Wayne got an opportunity to become a "singing cowboy."

television recognition as Sam the bartender for Kitty at the Long Branch Saloon on *Gunsmoke*.

One of the cast members in *Song of the Gringo* was Al Jennings, (the old, real-life Oklahoma outlaw) playing a judge. Jennings coached Tex, who was issued a fancy two-gun rig, on the fine points of fast draw and gun handling. The final cut of Tex's first film was sixty-two minutes and was released on November 22, 1936. Reviews were good. Various sources proclaimed Tex Ritter to be "a sensational new cowboy singing star."

The next picture was *Headin' for the Rio Grande*, and it was released less than a month after *Song of the Gringo*. The director was Robert N. Bradbury, father of B-Western star Bob Steele. As a veteran director of westerns, Bradbury worked on four films in the first *Range Rider* series. Another old pro, Gus Peterson, was cameraman for the first ten Tex Ritter movies. The new leading lady was pretty Eleanor Stewart, in this her first starring role. She caught on quickly, and worked as a leading lady for the next nine years. She played opposite Bob Steele, Ken Maynard, and Hopalong Cassidy, as well as several other not so-well-known cowboy stars.

Perhaps Tex had just won a fist fight — at least those swinging saloon doors look as if they took a beating.

For the third Tex Ritter movie, *Arizona Days*, the cast and crew traveled to Wilcox, Arizona for location shooting. It expected today that a film about Arizona would be shot there or include footage shot in Arizona, but in those days it was uncommon for studios to indulge such an expense. Tex co-wrote three of the songs for *Arizona Days*, as he had co-wrote three of the songs for *Headin' for the Rio Grande* which was released on December 20, 1936 to solid reviews.

By the end of 1936 Tex had made three movies, completed his first promotional tour, and recorded music from his films. Soon he would begin work on *Trouble in Texas*, destined to be one of his best films. And there would be another personal appearance tour. After just four months in Hollywood, Tex Ritter had experienced a major career leap, and 1937 promised more excitement and fame.

The leading lady in *Trouble in Texas* soon would become a superstar. She was billed as Rita Cansino, but her real name was Marquerita Carmen Cansino. Her mother and father were professional dancers and Rita began appearing with the Dancing Cansinos when she was just a little girl. A vivacious brunette, she moved with grace and an unconscious seductiveness, and in 1935 she began her film

*Glenn Strange was a great bad guy. He is remembered by modern generations as "Sam" on TV's **Gunsmoke**.*

career. Half of her ten movies as Rita Cansino were westerns, and *Trouble in Texas* was the last picture she made before changing her name to Rita Hayworth. Later she changed her hair color to red, and by the 1940s Rita Hayworth was one of Hollywood's biggest stars. Because of her box-office appeal, Trouble in Texas was re-released during the 1940s with Rita Hayworth advertised as the star.

Rita was just eighteen years old when *Trouble in Texas* was lensed and the beautiful young woman was positioned opposite Tex as a leading lady named Carmen (which just happened to be her real middle name). She portrayed an undercover government agent disguised as a dancer, and during one of the film's highlights she performed a superb saloon dance. *Variety* usually ignored the actresses who played heroines in B-Westerns, but its reviewer said, "Perhaps the best looker of all the girls working in hoss pics to date is Grand National's, Rita Cansino, she classes up the company she's in."

Tex soon learned that in his first full year in Hollywood making westerns had made him one of the most popular stars in town. During his first Hollywood year Tex made the "Top Ten list" of moneymakers among cowboy stars.

Can you see the resemblance to Tex's actor-son, John Ritter?

Tex was sixth on the list and he would make the list seven times in the next nine years. Tex never reached the Number-One status of Gene Autry or Roy Rogers, but he quickly built and maintained strong fan support.

THE 1937 TOP TEN COWBOY STARS

TOTAL POINTS

1. Gene Autry 946
2. William Boyd 941
3. Buck Jones 783
4. Dick Foran 733
5. George O'Brien 687
6. Tex Ritter 593
7. Three Mesquiteers 586
8. Charles Starrett 583
9. Ken Maynard 567
10. Bob Steele 554

1938 would see the demise of Grand National Studios. Under a release agreement, Tex had to make two more

Looks like Charlie King is being read the riot act by Tex.

films for Grand National. Tex made **_Rollin' Plains_** and the final Grand National film, **_Utah Trail_**. According to the storyline of the second film, cattle rustlers made use of an elusive "ghost train." The storyline for this film was supplied by Tex. A railroad siding was found in Bakersfield, CA for a day of shooting, and four days were spent at Chatham Ranch. During the film Tex sang tenderly to White Flash, "...there's no cow like a pony, a joggin' prairie crony."

After filming of **_Utah Trail_**, Tex's last film obligation to Grand National, he had to make a court appearance (June of '38) to finalize his contract cancellation with that studio. On July 8, 1938, **_Rollin' Plains_** was released. It was the first Tex Ritter movie in four months, and only the second in the past eight months. But within four days, on July 12, **_Utah Trail_** was shipped to the theaters.

Grand National tried to reorganize under new leadership while continuing to produce cheaper and cheaper films. The studio promoted Dorothy Page as the **_Singin' Cowgirl_**, but the idea of a female heroine was too alien for the time, and her series of musical westerns lasted for only three films. By 1940, Grand National was defunct. Tex

Marquerita Carmen Cansino, later known as Rita Hayworth.

Ritter had made twelve pictures for this studio before he headed over to Monogram Pictures.

Monogram Pictures started releasing films in 1931. The next year it released an impressive thirty-two films. Its western lineup included Tim McCoy, Bob Steele and Rex Bell — and in 1933 John Wayne came to Monogram for a two-year stint. Most of his sixteen films were written and directed by Robert N. Bradbury, father of John Wayne's boyhood friend, Bob Steele.

By the time Tex Ritter was heading to Monogram, Tom Keene and Jack Randall were Monogram's principal western stars. Keene was eventually dropped, and although Jack Randall was signed for another series of eight westerns, he never captured the public's imagination. Randall was the brother of *The Three Mesquiteers* star Bob Livingston. In 1942 Randall joined the Air Force, rising to the rank of captain by the time of his 1945 discharge. Jack immediately returned to moviemaking, but in July 1945 he was fatally injured in a fall from a horse while filming a serial about the Canadian Mounties.

The Pioneers, released on May 10,1941, completed Tex Ritter's current contract obligation to Monogram, as well

Gene Autry was ranked as the #1 cowboy star of 1937.

as his five-year contract with Ed Finney. He starred in thirty-two westerns produced by Finney — the last twenty for Monogram. Finney had brought Tex to Hollywood, but after a promising start, Tex's film career had stagnated. The first successful singing cowboy, Gene Autry, was the perennial leader of the Top Ten Western Stars. Roy Rogers, who did not star in a western musical until 1938 — two years after Tex Ritters' screen debut — saw his career rapidly gain momentum with Roy becoming the second most popular of the singing cowboys.

Tex Ritter was the third most popular singing cowboy, but in 1941 he finished only tenth among the Top Ten Western Stars, while Roy Rogers finished third. Autry and Rogers benefited from large budgets and Republic Studios' expertise. Autry and Rogers also benefited most by having faithful sidekicks. Smiley Burnette was a great asset to Gene Autry's success. And don't you think George "Gabby" Hayes helped Roy Rogers career — not to mention Dale Evans and Trigger. Where do you think Roy Rogers would have been without those three?

After leaving Monogram Pictures and longtime producer Ed Finney, Tex soon found a new celluloid home with a major studio — Columbia Pictures. The studio was found-

Tex was ranked as the #10 cowboy star of 1941, but the third most popular singing cowboy.

ed as a Poverty Row outfit in 1920 by Harry and Jack Cohen and Joe Brandt. Originally called CBC for Cohn-Brandt-Cohn, it soon got the nickname "Corn Beef and Cabbage" so the studio was renamed Columbia in 1924. Columbia produced more B-films, including westerns, than any other major studio.

Columbia's western stars were Wild Bill Elliott and Charles Starrett, neither of who sang on screen. Republic Studios dominated B-westerns with singing cowboys Gene Autry and Roy Rogers, but Columbia intended to compete in the western musical field and employed Tex Ritter. Tex signed with Columbia as a contract player. At Grand National and Monogram, Tex had been paid on a per picture basis, but as a Columbia contract player his weekly salary almost doubled his annual motion picture income.

There was, however, a major draw back to working with Columbia. The studio decided to co-star Tex in a series with Wild Bill Elliott. A third featured role, was a sidekick called "Cannonball," played by Dub Taylor. Trio-westerns was popularized by Hopalong Cassidy, Lucky Jenkins and California Carson (played by William Boyd, Russell Hayden and Andy Clyde). Tex Ritter's first film for

Columbia was well received by the movie audiences when released on August 14, 1941. Tex quickly became identified onscreen with his striking white stallion. But in reality, White Flash actually was a succession of white horses – whatever animal was available to rent when a Tex Ritter movie was being filmed.

In 1941 Tex bought a young, white stallion from Jerome Eddy of Chino Valley, Arizona. Eddy was a family friend of the Southworth family of Prescott, Arizona — which included the future Mrs. Tex Ritter. Tex hired noted trainer Glen Randall (who trained Trigger and, later Rex Allen's Koko) to train the new White Flash. As a result, Tex rode his own horse in later movies and on personal-appearance tours —where the horse was a big hit. One of the single-most important elements of the B-westerns was the hero's horse.

The immensely popular Tony — Tom Mix's "Wonder Horse" —received his own fan mail. One letter arrived at the Mix ranch simply addressed: "Just Tony, Somewhere in the U.S.A." William S. Hart rode a horse called Fritz — a smart horse that delighted fans with an assortment of tricks. Buck Jones was identified with Silver, Hopalong Cassidy with Topper, and Ken Maynard, a superb rider in

Smiley Burnette.

his own right, with Tarzan. Among the singing cowboys, Gene Autry would ride Champion and Roy Rogers galloped astride a magnificent palomino Trigger through all eighty-eight of his movies and each of his one hundred-and one television shows.

Tex declined to pick up the option on his contract with Columbia and grabbed the opportunity to sign with Universal. Tex hoped to revive his once-promising movie career at a new studio, but that never came about. At Universal Tex got stuck again with co-staring roles similar to those he had at Columbia. This time he was teamed with another cowboy star Johnny Mack Brown.

In 1945 Tex Ritter filmed his final movie as a singing cowboy. But in January of the same year, Tex established an enviable standard for country recording artists. The January 1945, issue of **Billboard** magazine announced that three Tex Ritter recordings were ranked "One, Two, and Three" on the country charts: *I'm Wastin' My Tears on You*, *There's a New Moon Over My Shoulder*, and *Jealous Heart*. Tex was the first country singer to monopolize the top-three position at the same time, and he became a Capital recording artist for as long as he would live — a total of thirty-two years.

Tom Mix and Tony the "Wonder Horse."

TR-19-23.

If his movie career was not what it might have been, it nevertheless developed a legion of Tex Ritter fans that would loyally support him for three decades. The little boy riding his broomstick pony around his yard in Murvaul, Texas had become a two-gun western hero astride his magnificent white stallion White Flash.

Tex rode his splendid mount during the last years of his music career and he often took White Flash on tour with him. For more than a decade Tex hauled White Flash to rodeos and fairs and parades, riding astride a beautifully decorated saddle. Tex also led White Flash on-stage, where the animal would perform tricks and then execute a bow to the audience.

The team of Tex Ritter and White Flash became as well known throughout rural America as Tom Mix and Tony had to an earlier generation of cowboy fans. Tex retired White Flash in 1953 to the Lazy TNT. But two years later he sold the little ranch, and White Flash was pastured in Bouquet Canyon near Kernville, where Tex had filmed movies—nearly a hundred miles north of Los Angeles.

Rex Allen, who had become the last of the singing cowboys in 1950, ran mares on a ranch in Bouquet. He had

Tex, like many cowboy stars, had more than one horse that appeared as "his" mount, White Flash.

noticed an old white horse in a pasture. One day Allen recognized Tex Ritter, "talking soft and low, while the horse stood with his head over Tex's shoulder." Allen observed, "a comradeship that you see only when a horse and a man come to mean a lot to each other over the years." Allen was impressed. "The fact that he had traveled a hundred miles or so over busy weekend freeways just to talk to that horse told me what kind of man Tex Ritter really was."

Woodard Maurice Ritter, better known to us as "Tex," left us on January 2, 1974. He died in Nashville—a place that he helped make even more famous with more contemporary western tunes such as ***Rye Whiskey***, ***Boll Weevil***, ***Wayward Wind***, ***Hillbilly Heaven***, ***You Are My Sunshine***, and the famous theme from ***High Noon***. He had a loving marriage to Dorothy Fay (married in 1941) and had two sons. He served as president of the Country Music Hall of Fame for three years in the 60's and even made an unsuccessful attempt for the U.S. Senate from Tennessee in 1970. He will remain one of the great western personalities to ever grace the silver screen.

In life…all good things have to come to an end…So Long, White Flash…So Long Tex…There they go down the moonlit trail…but they'll return…soon again…no need to say good-bye…..until then…So Long White Flash…So Long Tex…until we meet again.

Thanks For the Memories,

Tex and White Flash

For The Exciting Adventures In My Happy Days of Youth

CHAPTER 7

THE PEACEABLE MAN

"WILD" BILL ELLIOTT

"BY NATURE I'M A PEACEABLE MAN." Those words were the trademark of one of the best cowboy stars to ever come out of Hollywood: Wild Bill Elliott. He spoke those words in many of his western movies. I can still hear Little Beaver, as if it was yesterday, saying: "Red Ryder, him peaceable man." Those words were synonymous with Bill Elliott — just as wearing his six-guns in a reversed fashion.

Bill Elliott was born Gordon Nance on a ranch outside Pattonsburg, Missouri in 1905. Bill's childhood hero was William S. Hart the silent screen cowboy star. He learned to understand and love horses at an early age, and rode his

*Elliott displayed his famous smile in this **Red Ryder** promotional shot.*

first horse at the age of five. In his teenage years Bill became a top rodeo performer, taking first place in the American Royal Horse and Livestock Show at the age of sixteen. Many of his wins were in competition with adult cowboys. When the family moved to Kansas City young Elliott spent much of his spare time hanging with the cowboys around the stockyards where his father was the commission man. It was at these stockyards that he learned the art of riding, roping, bulldogging, and bronco busting from the best teachers he could have had — real cowboys.

At the age of nine, after seeing William S. Hart on the screen, Bill wanted to become a movie cowboy. (Later in his career it was rumored that he would portray Hart in a movie about the star's life; but that never materialized.) Bill's mother, according to reports, once told him that a fortune teller had told her that he was going to be a Hollywood movie star someday, and this was one of the reasons Bill left for Hollywood after high school and attending Rockingham College.

Bill Elliott was a tall, lean and ruggedly handsome man. In California he enrolled at the Pasadena Community Playhouse where he was spotted and signed by a studio

In addition to a great smile, Elliott could give the opposition a tremendous stern poker face.

1148-99

scout to play, of all things, in society dramas. Bill, being a westerner at heart, was very disappointed, but he stuck it out for over eight years.

During this period, his name was changed from Gordon Nance to Gordon Elliott. His first film was *The Plastic Age* (made in 1925), which featured Clara Bow and Gilbert Roland. At this same period of time in his career he appeared with some of the biggest names in the business: Joe E. Brown, Al Jolson, James Cagney, Pat O'Brien, Bette Davis, Edward G. Robinson, and Jackie Cooper.

He did manage to get into a western or two during this time: *Trailin' West, Guns of the Pecos*, and *Moonlight on the Prairie* with cowboy star Dick Foran at Warner Brothers. He also got to play the lead villain in *Roll Along Cowboy* opposite Smith Ballew at Fox Studios and lead the villain again opposite Gene Autry in *Boots And Saddles* at Republic Studios.

In 1938, two years after making his first western, Elliott starred in the very popular Columbia serial *The Great Adventures of Wild Bill Hickok*. Wild Bill Hickok wore his six-shooters with the butts forward, and the reversed six-gun style later became the trademark of Wild Bill

Elliott. In his first western feature for Columbia, his name was changed from Gordon Elliott to Bill Elliott. Throughout his career at Columbia, he would be billed as Bill Elliott, and only when he went to Republic Studios was he billed as "Wild Bill Elliott."

Elliott went on to star in twenty-four westerns for Columbia Studios. Columbia also had at the time another well-known cowboy star by the name of Charles Starrett (who made more western movies than any other cowboy star). Starrett made all of his one hundred-and-thirty-one western films for Columbia. In more than half of his films he portrayed the "Durango Kid" — a hero of justice that wore a black outfit with a black mask who sat astride a big beautiful white stallion named Raider.

In Columbia's westerns, Elliott portrayed *Wild Bill Hickok*. In six of the eight movies that he co-starred with Tex Ritter, Elliott played Hickok. Columbia produced more B-Movies, including westerns than any other major studio, and their top western stars were Wild Bill Elliott and Charles Starrett. At the time however, Republic Studios dominated the B-Western market with their two giant stars — the two singing cowboys, Gene Autry and Roy Rogers.

Duded up in one of the outfits that he felt most uncomfortable wearing.

Columbia soon decided to compete in the western musical field and they signed singing cowboy star Tex Ritter. "Trio Westerns" were very popular at this time (such as the *Hopalong Cassidy* series at Paramount Studios, and The *Three Mesquiteer*s series at Republic Studios. So after signing Tex Ritter, Columbia teamed Tex up with Wild Bill Elliott, with Dub Taylor in the third featured role, playing the comedy sidekick "Cannonball." Dub Taylor became a well-known character actor in movies and on television. His son, Buck Taylor, played Newly on the television series *Gunsmoke*.

The other studios imitated the "Trio Westerns" with the likes of: Buck Jones, Tim McCoy and Raymond Hatton in the *Rough Riders* series. And there was Ken Maynard, Hoot Gibson and Bob Steele in the *Trail Blazers* series. And finally, there was Ray Corrigan, Dennis Moore and Max Terhune in the *Range Busters* series.

Tex Ritter was accustomed to starring in his own series, and once he became a trio co-star he would find it difficult to regain his individual stardom. Elliott no more wanted to be relegated to co-star status than did Ritter. By 1942, Elliott rose to seventh place among the Top Ten Western Stars — his highest finish to date. Co-starring

"Wild" Bill Elliott was Red Ryder.

with Tex Ritter apparently boosted Elliott's career, but he had no intention of continuing to share Columbia's screen with anyone.

Bill Elliott, a self-proclaimed peaceable man, was always prepared to battle the bad guys. Perhaps he was beast known for his many portrayals of the comic book character Red Ryder and his movie nickname "Wild Bill." In 1943 Elliott left Columbia for the Republic Studios—the best in the business, at the time, at making B-Westerns. Republic starred Elliott most notably in **Red Ryder**, and by 1946 he had risen to second place in the Top Ten (just behind Roy Rogers). During his career he would finish in the Top Ten of Money Making Western Stars fifteen times. Only Gene Autry and Roy Rogers topped that with sixteen times each. Bill Elliott did share the screen again, however this time it was with Bobby Blake who played the little Indian boy called Little Beaver. Bobby Blake would also later play Little Beaver in the **Red Ryder** series that starred Allan "Rocky" Lane.

Bill Elliott had quite a few sidekicks in his westerns while at Republic Studios. He would saddle up with George "Gabby" Hayes in two **Red Ryder** films (**Tucson Raiders** and **Marshal of Reno**) and eight other non-Ryder films.

Studio publicity shot.

The San Antonio Kid, released in August of 1944 was Bill Elliott's third film in the *Red Ryder* series and his eleventh for Republic Studios. Gabby Hayes was not in *The San Antonio Kid*. It was the first Republic Elliott film that Gabby Hayes had not been apart of the cast. Earle Hodgins would play the sidekick role in this film, but disappeared from the later *Red Ryder* films. He appeared in the *Hopalong Cassidy* series from 1944 through 1948.

In 1946, the year Hopalong Cassidy was seen in only one picture — *The Devil's Playground* — which was released in November. This time Bill Elliott teamed up with, my favorite Hoppy sidekick, Andy Clyde, in *Plainsman and the Lady*, by Republic. Andy and Bill worked well together and would have made a great team, however in 1946 Andy Clyde returned to the *Hopalong Cassidy* series to become the comic California Carlson once again.

Unlike Bill Elliott, Tex Ritter's year as a co-star dropped him from the ranks of the top ten. With Elliott gone, Tex declined to pick up the option on his contract with Columbia for another year and quickly signed with Universal Studios. All Tex had accomplished was to go from one co-starring role to another. At Universal he would co-star with another famous cowboy actor of the

Emmett Lynn peers out from between Bill's legs, while Jay Kirby stands in the doorway in **Plainsman and the Lady** *(1946).*

day, the ever-popular Johnny Mack Brown — the former All-American football star from the University of Alabama who turned western star at Universal Studios. At Universal, Tex Ritter was promised some roles in which he wouldn't have to co-star with some other name. The promise was kept and he did make two pictures as the star, however, because of a health problem he didn't get to make the third one.

Before finishing *Valley of Vanishing Men* serial for Columbia, Bill Elliott had negotiated a contract with Republic Studios. Republic first starred Elliott in a series of eight westerns with Gabby Hayes and Anne Jeffreys. He used his own name in this series and from the first, *Calling Wild Bill Elliott* (1943) to the last picture of the series *Hidden Valley Outlaws*. They all had good plots and a lot of fast action. This was probably the best western series of Elliott's career, the Tex Ritter series being a close second. In one of the pictures Alice Fleming, who later would play the Duchess in the Red Ryder series, portrayed the head villain in the *Overland Mail Robbery*. Kirk Alyn, later to play *Superman* for Columbia Studios, was also cast in this film.

After that series, Republic decided to revive their *Red Ryder* property, starring Don "Red" Barry in the 1940 serial. Wild Bill Elliott's most popular series was *Red Ryder* (Republic), that starred Bobby Blake and Alice Fleming (as the Duchess in all sixteen Red Ryder films) and sometimes George "Gabby" Hayes. Others appearing in the series included: Peggy Stewart, Monte Hale, Rex Lease, Bob Steele, Allan Lane, and Roy Barcroft.

With a couple of *Red Ryder* features to go of the sixteen, Republic decided to move Bill Elliott up to their "A" western productions and cast him in *In Old Sacramento*. The picture was a success. And after finishing *Sun Valley Cyclone* and *Conquest of Cheyenne* — both 1946 successful *Red Ryder* features, Bill's name was changed to William Elliott. And from that moment forward, he was cast in Republic's "A" western productions. A total of ten films were produced in this series — two of them being filmed in the new Trucolor: *Hellfire* and *The Last Bandit*. Some sources said Bill wanted out of the *Red Ryder* series. Others have said he was reluctant to leave and didn't want to do the "A" series. I believe he always wanted to do bigger western productions — on the level of John Wayne westerns. Think about it, after sixteen *Red Ryder* features, what else could be done with the Ryder character?

The great George "Gabby" Hayes born George "Francis" Hayes in 1885.

Bill proved to be a better actor in this series than some had expected. *Hellfire, The Gallant Legion, In Old Sacramento*, and *The Showdown* were the best of this series. *The Showdown* was an excellent western. And for those of you young whippersnappers who didn't think B-Western cowboys could act, you need to get yourself a video of this feature and watch it. Bill Elliott, like William Boyd, had several years acting under their belts before either one of them starred in cowboy westerns.

Like all the other cowboys, Bill Elliott had his horse — a beautiful black stallion called Thunder. He appeared with Elliott in all of his *Red Ryder* films. Because a horse was so very important to the cowboy star, it was hard to find a horse to play the role of Thunder. Most cowboys loved their horses and asked a lot of them. The horse had to have a nice disposition; it had to be able to run at a tremendous speed; and when he came to a close-up, the animal had to remain quiet so not to interfere with the dialogue.

After looking over forty or fifty black horses he selected the one he rode in the *Red Ryder* series. Thunder was one of the most beautiful of all the motion picture cowboy

Andy Clyde was born in Scotland in 1892 and became one of the great sidekicks and appeared in 244 films during his career.

horses. He was 15 1/2 hands tall and weighed 1,150 pounds. Elliott bought him from Levi Garret of Sterling City, Texas and the stallion traveled with Elliott all over the United States. In his spare time he would take Thunder to children's hospitals and entertain the boys and girls that could not get out and run, play, and ride like the other kids. When Elliott took Thunder into the hospital wards, he didn't even put a halter on him. Thunder would walk in-and-around the kids just as carefully as could be, while letting them sit on him. He would sometimes have as many as six kids on his back at one time.

Thunder was one of the finest horses any cowboy could ever hope to own. And Elliott took good care of the horse and was very protective of what he was fed. Elliott never gave him sugar because he didn't think sugar was good for him. Thunder's favorite treat was carrots. They kept his hair shinny and balanced out his diet. Thunder also had a special mixture of grain that Elliott had concocted and which was given to him at every meal.

At every rodeo performance Elliott would ride into the arena on Thunder and show him off by executing a series of tricks. Thunder would dance, push a baby buggy, pick

Anne Jeffreys appeared with Gabby Hayes in **Calling Wild Bill Elliott** *made in 1943.*

up Elliott's hat off the ground and give it to him. Thunder would sit down and Elliott would put on the animal's special glasses while he would hold the funny paper in his mouth. Thunder would go to the mailbox and bring the mail to Bill. And finally, he would always "say" his prayers.

Elliott had a special horse trailer made to carry Thunder and his quarter horse stallion, Stormy Night (which Elliott would also ride in every rodeo performance). Stormy and Thunder were always kept stabled next to each other, they became good friends, and they did not like to be separated.

Bill Elliott personally stood out because of his rugged good looks and his wardrobe. Bill wore one of the most outstanding outfits of all the stars. I loved the fringed buckskin outfit that he topped off with one of the best looking hats among all the western cowboys. Bill also wore chaps when playing Red Ryder, and was, in my opinion, just about the best western outfit any cowboy ever wore in movies.

Most of all, I loved Bill's riding ability and his horses. Sonny, a black and white, was ridden in his first series of

*The future TV detective Tony Baretta (Bobby Blake) strikes a pose as "Little Beaver" with Elliott and Hayes in a promotional shot for the **Red Ryder** series.*

westerns. Sonny was a high-spirited horse and showed off Bill's true riding talents. Bill also rode that beautiful black stallion, Thunder when filming the ***Red Ryder*** series. Bill had a nice, easy going manner — he was a peaceable man. He could handle himself well in action scenes, making him the most believable cowboy hero ever. Bill Elliott worked hard at being a believable cowboy. He was highly capable; he worked at, practiced, studied, and rehearsed his craft.

After completing the last film in the William Elliott series, ***The Showdown***, Bill left Republic Studios and signed on to do a series for Monogram Pictures (later to become called Allied Artists Pictures). Although this series didn't have the polish and budgets behind it as the Republic productions, they did have good scripts and a realistic appearance. Starting with ***The Longhorn*** (1951), Bill made eleven pictures in this series. It was in this series that he came close to emulating William S. Hart — that of a bad man going straight. Elliott again picked up the "Wild Bill" in the billing for this series. The pictures were probably a step down from his Republic "A" pictures, and just a little above the average B-Western.

Bill Elliott astride Thunder.

After finishing *The Forty Niners* in 1954, Bill's western film career came to an end. With television taking over much of the B-Western movie market, virtually every other western series had folded their tents — with the exception of the Wayne Morris series that was also shot at Allied Artists (but it soon came to the trails end as well).

Bill did five detective features for Allied Artists. Not as good as Bill's westerns, the detective series was entertaining. But with *Footsteps in the Night*, released in 1957, Bill Elliott's movie career ended. A long and successful career that started back in 1925 was finally over.

Bill moved to Las Vegas two years before his death. From his ranch in northern Nevada he conducted a weekly TV show, during which he would interview personalities and show one of his old western films. On November 26, 1965, Bill died of cancer. He had been hospitalized at Sunrise Hospital for nearly four weeks before being released. Another one of our great American cowboy heroes was called home to the big range in the sky. His passing brought to an end the career of "The Peaceable Man" who had entertained fans for nearly three decades.

THE PEACEABLE MAN

Oh, I knew you so well but we never met,
but the memories of you I'll never forget.

Straight forward and honest but most of all,
you and your principles always stood tall.

Each Saturday morning around about nine,
eager to get in I would be standing in line.

Once I was seated and the lights were low,
my heart would stop beating, my pulse would slow,
and I'd ride the range with Little Beaver and you,
chase the bad guys and give them their due.

With all the risks you took, the dangers and falls,
I was right there beside you and shared them all.

As Hickok and Saunders, Ryder and the rest,
there was no one better, for you were the best.

In my youth you gave me memories and pleasures,
that I wouldn't trade for all of earth's treasures.

When it was time to right a wrong you took a stand,
and I never will forget you as the "Peaceable Man."

Poem by Dolores Worley Reams

But like in life...all good things have to come to an end...So-long Thunder...So-long Wild Bill...There they go...down the moonlit trail...but they will return...soon again...no need to say good-bye...until then...So-long Thun-der...So-long Peaceable Man...until we meet again.

Thanks For the Memories,

Wild Bill and Thunder

For The Exciting Adventures In My Happy Days of Youth

THE GALLANT DEFENDER

CHARLES

" THE DURANGO KID"

STARRETT

REMEMBER THOSE THRILLING SATURDAY AFTERNOONS at the local movie house when we were kids? I sure do. Whenever we could scrap up a dime or two we would be right there, down town at the local theatre, like everyone else that could find a dime, to watch

the most remarkable colorful western cowboy star that ever rode across the silver screen. His name was Charles Starrett, aka ***The Durango Kid***. This remarkable silver-screen cowboy starred in over one hundred-and-thirty Western films — thanks to Columbia Studios!

Today the range is silent;
tranquility reigns over the land.
Even the bad guys pay tribute to
a just and wonderful man.
Today hearts were broken;
today grown men cried.
Another saddle is now empty,
for today Durango died.
I thought he would live forever-
at least I hoped he would-
for today we need a hero
to teach us how to do good.
Perhaps God likes horses
and tired riding alone,
so for companionship
he called Durango home.

Poem by Bobby J. Copeland

Collage of Charles Starrett and his alter-ego
"The Durango Kid."

So, How about it! Don't you think it is time to unlock the vaults and let Charles Starrett and the Durango Kid... *Take Us Back To Those Wide Open Spaces* and let us live our lives over once again?!

Legendary Western actor Charles Starrett, who rose to stardom as the cowboy hero The Durango Kid, died in California March 22, 1986, just a few days short of his eighty-third birthday. Starrett was legally blind and suffered from a heart condition for several years. However, he remained very alert and even appeared at a Western film festival in North Carolina in 1984. Only shortly before his death was he diagnosed with terminal cancer.

Charles Starrett was born March 28, 1903 in Athol, Massachusetts. His grandfather was the founder of the famed F. S. Starrett Tool Company. Starrett graduated from Dartmouth College in 1926 where he had excelled in swimming and football. Dartmouth turned down an invitation to play in The Rose Bowl in 1926, and the University of Alabama got the invitation. As a result, Johnny Mack Brown became the MVP of the Rose Bowl — an outstanding game against the University of Washington in which Alabama beat their rivals 20-19.

Studio magic as Starrett and "the Kid" shake hands.

Brown later ended up with a movie contract with MGM and went on to become a western star in his own right.

In 1930 Charles Starrett embarked on his movie career, and along with his good friend Boris Karloff, was one of the founders of the Screen Actors Guild. Columbia Studios groomed Charles Starrett to replace the great cowboy star Tim McCoy. Starrett made his Western film debut in Stampede — a thrilling sagebusher in which an evil rancher murders a rival rancher to get his land. The incident prompts the rancher's brother (played by Starrett) to search for the killer. Starrett would continue as a western star for Columbia Studios for the next seventeen years — a record for a star at one studio.

Charles Starrett was synonymous with The Durango Kid, a character he portrayed in over sixty films. His portrayal of Durango — a "good guy" who wore black (including a mask) and who was a paragon of virtue, was one of the longest-running characterizations in Hollywood history (next to William Boyd's *Hopalong Cassidy* with sixty-six feature films). The Durango Kid was a combination of The Lone Ranger and Zorro all rolled into one. Columbia introduced the masked rider in a 1940 film,

Not a man to be messed with.

properly named *The Durango Kid*. However, it was not until 1945 that they decided to continue the series. Starrett, tall and handsome, cut a dashing figure on his beautiful white horse Raider. And interestingly, he was the only actor to ever play the Durango role.

Lester Alvin "Smiley" Burnette, the comedian who was billed as "The West's No. 1 Comic," was the principal sidekick in the Durango films.

Starrett was the hero in one hundred-and-thirty-two Western films. He was consistently voted among the top ten moneymaking Western actors and once was voted Hollywood's most-handsome cowboy star. In addition to his friendship with Boris Karloff, one of his closest friends and hunting companions was another Johnny Mack Brown. During some of their hunting trips, I wonder if the 1926 Rose Bowl ever came up?

It was unfortunate that Starrett decided to retire in 1952 at the early age of 48. And it is equally unfortunate that Columbia has not released *The Durango Kid* films. Many feel that if Starrett had chosen to enter TV, and if Columbia had released the films, he would have attained

One of the most handsome faces in the Columbia stable.

the popularity that Hopalong Cassidy, Roy Rogers and Gene Autry did through their TV exposure. Charles Starrett lived a superlative lifestyle with his wife of nearly sixty years, the former Mary McKinnon. His many fans miss this charming actor. He was a warm, gracious gentleman and greatly respected by all who knew him. He was one cowboy star who lived up to the image that he depicted on the silver screen.

Starrett was often asked why he went from straight roles into making strictly Westerns. At first he did not like being typecast as a cowboy all the time. But the films were making money and he was making money. Later on he said he was glad that he had done it!

Jimmy Wakely and Dub Taylor often played Starrett's sidekicks. After one of Starrett's movie fights there would typically be a musical interlude featuring Jimmy Wakely and the Sunshine Boys. Wakely born in Mineola, AK, became one of the most popular Western singers of his day. As part of the Wakely Trio, he was heard on an Oklahoma City-radio station by Gene Autry who signed the group to come to Hollywood as guest of his *Melody Ranch Show*.

"The Durango Kid" with sidekick Smiley Burnette.

Jimmy Wakely appeared in many Westerns as musical backup to non-singing cowboys such as Hopalong Cassidy, Bill Elliott, Johnny Mack Brown and Charles Starrett, before getting a series of his own at Monogram Pictures. By 1962 Jimmy Wakely had sold over 15 million records Remember these big hits? I sure do: **Slipping Around** and **One Has My Name**. Perhaps Jimmy's best recording was a Christmas duet with Margaret Whiting entitled **Silver Bells**.

Jimmy Wakely died of heart failure in 1982, at the age of sixty-eight, after suffering a long bout with asthma. Starrett liked Jimmy and they worked well together, but Starrett said Jimmy smoked too much. Starrett would say to Jimmy, "Jimmy see if you can't cut back." Jimmy would always reply, "It doesn't bother me; it doesn't bother me."

In **Saddle Leather Law**, Charles called his horse Yucca, after the white desert wild flower. The execs at Columbia said, "No, no. You can't name your horse that." The studio took a poll and the name of this beautiful white horse became Raider. In **Saddle Leather Law** the comedy side-kick to Starrett was Dub Taylor as Cannonball — the nickname the studio gave him after he began making westerns in the early 40s'.

The former Dartmouth grad who missed the 1926 Rose Bowl and gave Johnny Mack Brown a shot at the game's MVP.

Born Walter Taylor in Richmond, VA, Dub first attracted public attention with his harmonica and xylophone playing. A few years later, a vaudevillian named Larry Rich brought the youngster to New York where his high-cackle laugh and predisposition for a good time smoothed over the rough edges of his musical abilities. It was Dub's personality that prompted film director Frank Capra to cast him as Ed Carmichael in the movie *You Can't Take It With You* in 1938. Soon after that Columbia Pictures signed him as a contract player. A onetime sidekick to such Western greats as: Bill Elliott, Tex Ritter, Russell Hayden, as well as Charles Starrett, Dub Taylor continued to work in other motion pictures, TV shows and commercials.

Charles Starrett started making movies for Columbia Studios in 1935 and was constantly listed in the Top Ten Western Stars Money Making List. He would make the list fourteen times during his movie career — the same number of times as William Boyd. The only cowboys to make the list more times were William Elliott (fifteen times) and Gene Autry and Roy Rogers (sixteen times each).

 Singing cowboy Jimmy Wakely and comic relief Dub Taylor

Charles Starrett was stood 6' 2" and weighed in at 180 pounds. He was athletic and considered by many to be "the most handsome Western star." And on top of that, he was a decent actor. In 1940 he starred in what was assumed to be just another Columbia Western, a film entitled *The Durango Kid*. This role, however, was destined to change the course of his career. It also created one of the most popular western heroes of the silver screen.

In this film, Starrett played a dual role: young Bill Lowry, a ranch owner whose father had been murdered, and the masked Pecos gunsharp known as "The Durango Kid." In the end, Lowry avenges the death of his father. Good triumphed again over evil. This format drew tons and tons of mail from the youngsters who attended Saturday afternoon Westerns. Both fans and theatre owners alike wanted more of The Durango Kid!

It took Columbia Studios until 1945 to bow to the wishes of the public and release *The Return of The Durango Kid*. Plans were made to put Starrett into the role in much the same way William Boyd became his role — Hopalong Cassidy. The series was a tremendous success — in much the same way the Hoppy series had been for Paramount Studios. By the time the dust had settled in 1952, Starrett

"The Durango Kid" on Thunder.

had made sixty-five films in the Durango series—just one short of William Boyd's record of sixty-six films playing the same character. The *Hopalong Cassidy* and *The Durango Kid* Series were the two most colorful and exciting Western series ever made...not to mention, long-lasting.

One of the most amazing things about *The Durango Kid* series was that it seemed to get better as the series developed. Durango became more athletic as Starrett matured —thanks for the most part to Jock Mahoney's doubling as the masked rider. Even in his forties Starrett could dish out the action as I recently discovered while watching a Durango film (a rare event).

The Durango Kid films are as rare as hen's teeth due to the fact that Columbia Studios never released the series for television use. Many of the movies have never been seen since their initial theater runs. Private film collectors have kept the legend alive and proudly exhibit the films at national film festivals. When a new Durango Kid film turns up in the collector's market, it's a rare treat.

In each film, The Durango Kid always had the same first "civilian" name — "Steve" (always with a different last

Screen hero who went on to have a line of "Durango Kid" comic books.

name, from feature to feature). This was established in the film ***Texas Panhandle*** (1945) in which Steve was a Secret Service man working out west. This would explain how he might be a Texas Ranger in one film and a marshal in the next. In the comic books, Steve always had the same last name — Brand — and he had a sidekick named Muley Pike (a heavy set fellow that shared his adventures and confidence). Muley was based on the film character played by Smiley Burnette. ME only licensed Charles Starrett and The Durango Kid. Smiley had his own license going with another comic book company so he could not appear in The Durango Kid comic books.

The final entry in the series was ***The Kid From Broken Gun***, released in 1952. With that feature completed, Charles Starrett retired from the movie business. He was financially well off and during the 1950's and 1960's he traveled around the world with his lovely wife, Mary. In the early 1980's he attended a few Western film festivals, much to the delight of his fans. Early in 1986, he passed away.

In December of 1989, Jock Mahoney died. He was the other Durango Kid — since he doubled behind the black mask in many an action scene. Others intimately involved

Smiley Burnett on his horse Ringeye.

with The Durango Kid — writer Gardner Fox, artist Joe Certa and director Fred Sears — have all passed away as well.

As time marches on, and so many of our silver-screen heroes have left us, books become even more important to us and to the history of Westerns. It is collectors like myself, along with writers and publishers who have pre-served the legacy these fabulous cowboys have left us. It is an important legacy, and the older I get the more I find myself wishing for those wonderful days of the old Westerns again. There are grown men, including myself, who were guided through our lives to stay on the right path because of these cowboys — The Great Eight and all of the other Saturday-afternoon matinee heroes. So sad-dle up pals and ride again with "The Gallant Defender" in those wide-open spaces.

But in life...all good things...have to come to an end...So long Charlie...So long Raider...There they go...down the moonlit trail...but they will return soon again...no need to say good-bye...until then...So-long Charles Starrett...Durango Kid...So-long Raider...until we meet again!

Long way from Dartmouth College and his birthplace of Athol, Massachusetts.

3048.61

Thanks For the Memories,

Charlie and Raider

For The Exciting Adventures In My Happy Days of
Youth

Some "good guys" wore black.

CHAPTER 9

MICHELANGELO AND THE OUTLAW

BOB BROWN AND AL JENNINGS

IN MAY OF 1999, IN CAMBRIDGE, OHIO at the Hopalong Cassidy Film Festival, I met the most interesting person I have ever met in my entire life. The night before the festival was to begin, I was in the restaurant at the Holiday Inn, when Barry Tourtellotte spotted me seated at a table alone. He invited me over to his table to join him and many other festival attendees. A gentleman came into the restaurant, spoke to everyone and joined us. He was a tall fellow (close to my own height of 6' 4" or taller). I said to Barry, "He looks more like a cowboy than anyone I've seen so far." That's when I found out that he

Monte Hale (left) congratulating Bob Brown the new "honorary" mayor of Big Bear City, California (1981).

was Bob Brown from California. He was the man that made the gun holster worn by Hopalong Cassidy — the one I loved and want since I was a little tot — the one I hoped and prayed to get every Christmas — the one that never seem to find its way under the Christmas tree.

After dinner that night, Barry introduced me to Bob Brown. I found out that Bob and I had one thing in common besides cowboys. It was sports. Bob had played basketball and baseball at Pasadena Junior College. While playing baseball he played against Robert Taylor, the future movie star, who played on the Pomona College team. Bob also competed against Jackie Robinson, the great second basemen for the Brooklyn Dodgers. Baseball was my favorite sport, although I played all three major sports in school, baseball, basketball and football. As a young kid, my cowboy hero was Hopalong Cassidy, but as I grew older my hero became a baseball player — a player who not only played pro ball but also served his country during two wars. This made the man a larger-than-life-hero to me. His name was Ted Williams, *the splendid splinter*. People speak of achievements in baseball. The greatest was accomplished, in my opinion, by Williams when he hit .406 in 1941, went into the military, and returned to play a full season in 1946, leading the American League

A true artist and gentleman.

in batting average, homers and runs-batted-in (RBI's). I can't think of a player who could have left the game for that period of time and who wouldn't have been washed up as a result.

The next day the festival started and I had a great time meeting a lot of wonderful people. I also saw several people wearing my favorite Hopalong Cassidy gun holster. Bob Brown showed me one that he had made and I told him that I'd love to have one if he would make one for me —not knowing if he still could do that kind of meticulous work. Before the festival ended, Bob had agreed to make me a version of the Hoppy holster that I liked best of all the ones my hero had worn. Brown had made Hoppy five different holsters, but the one I liked best was black with silver and trimmed with white leather.

A few weeks after I got back home, a package arrived from Bob Brown. My wife and I opened it together (she was as anxious to see this item as I was). She had seen the holster many times on the videos I collect and was familiar with its appearance. When I pulled it from the box she said, "Oh my that is beautiful; it is gorgeous. This Bob Brown is an artist. I must say it is one fine piece of art." When I

Bob guarding his goldmine (in his backyard) in Big Bear.

phoned Bob to tell him how much I appreciated the great job, he told me that he felt it was the best one he had ever made.

Bob Brown had done some beautiful leather and silver work for Sunset Carson, Rex Allen, Gene Autry, Johnny Mack Brown, Charles Starrett, Allen "Rocky" Lane, Ray "Crash" Corrigan, Bob Livingston, and Hopalong Cassidy, to name a few. The "Michelangelo of Leather," that is Bob Brown of Hollywood, CA.

Bob Brown was a master craftsman. When the Alexander Dumas classic, the ***Man in the Iron Mask***, was being produced, the studio came to Bob Brown to inquire if he could make a mask out of leather that would look like iron (to be worn by Louis Hayward). Bob made the mask of leather loaded it with metal studs wherever he could put them. The leather was antiqued to give it that iron appearance. In the story, as you will recall, the twin — the king—was placed in a dungeon for life with the mask permanently riveted to his head. (The story also makes an interesting point that the king's beard almost suffocates him while growing inside the mask.) Viewers had no idea the mask they saw was made of leather.

*The author of **Those Wide Open Spaces**, Hank Williams, wearing his Bob Brown special-made holster.*

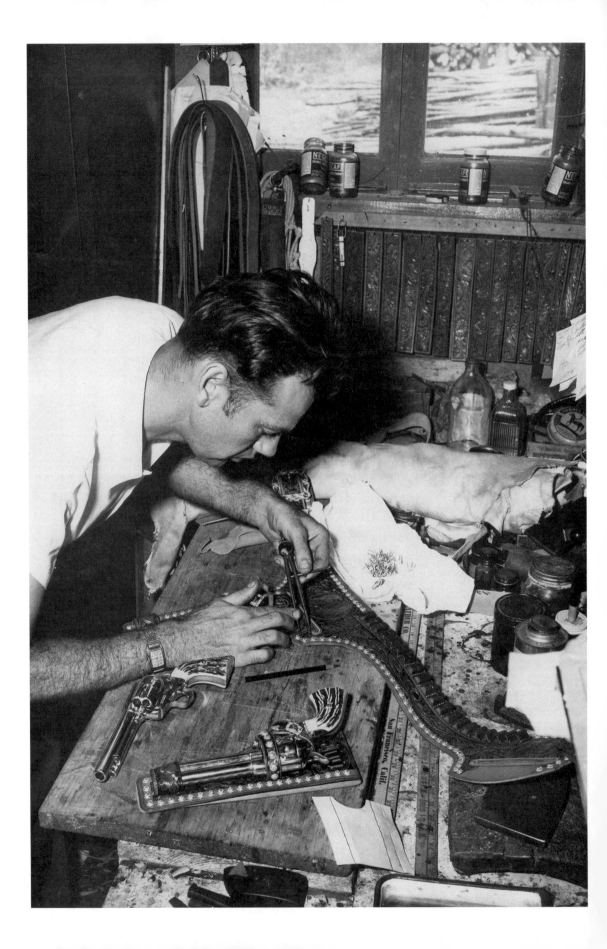

Another very interesting piece of work for which Bob was commissioned was for Boris Karloff, the ax man in the movie *Tower of London*. The studio came to Bob to create a pair of hideous boots for Boris to wear in the movie. Bob made the boot tops of beautiful maroon suede leather and the vamps of the reverse-side-out of saddle leather. He made the heel counters and side plates of copper and used brass studs to make the boots look as hideous as possible. In the movie, when Boris is caring his ax up the cobblestone steps of the Tower of London, the metal plate on the side of the boot made an exceptionally weird sound as it was drug along the stone.

If by some chance you didn't see *The Tower of London* or *Man in the Iron Mask*, you will, however, recognize another of Brown's creations — the logo for Columbia Pictures. Bob created that in 1931. Eagle Lion Studios got Bob to make all the leather needed in the making of the *Calgary Stampede*, which starred James Craig and Joan Leslie. He even did all the leatherwork for one of Hollywood's first movie cowboys — William S. Hart. On one visited by Bob and his wife Jolly to the William S. Hart's Museum in Newhall, California, they discovered that Hart was ill. His nurse told Bob and Jolly to come

Brown hard at work in his studio.
*(Notice the **Nescafe** instant coffee jars on the windowsill.)*

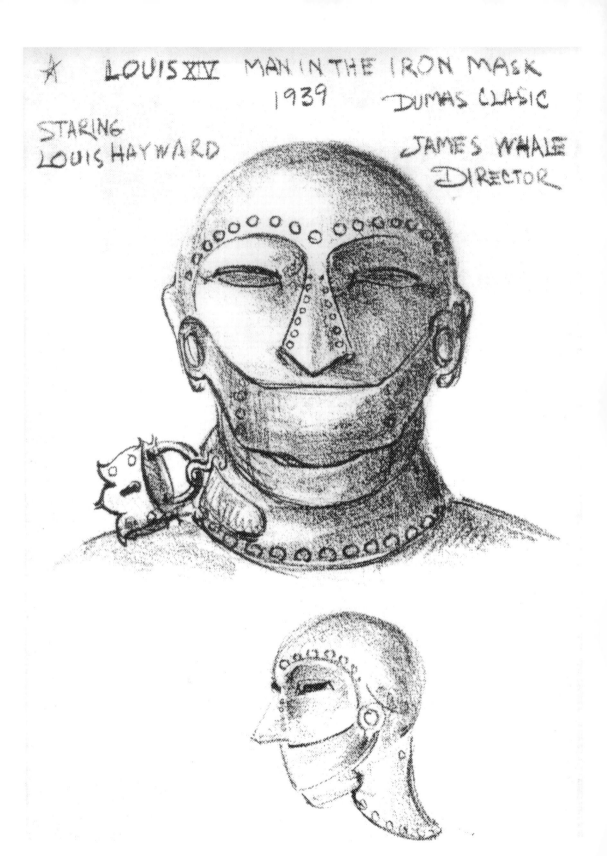

☆ LOUIS XIV MAN IN THE IRON MASK
1939   DUMAS CLASIC

STARING
LOUIS HAYWARD

JAMES WHALE
DIRECTOR

back the next day, suggesting tat he would be feeling much better. That night, the famous actor passed away.

Do you remember the movie called *They Died with Their Boots On*, starring Errol Flynn? Well, Bob loaned Flynn his own horse Don to ride in that movie. Bob also made the green costume worn by Flynn in the 1938 version of *The Adventures of Robin Hood*. Bob even made the pointed slippers Flynn wore. This costume was sold years later at auction for $33,000.

Buck Jones, one of the great screen cowboys, was a close friend of Bob's. Bob did some leatherwork for Buck and his wife Dell. Jones had a riding group called the Range Riders with whom he spent much of his personal time — not for the movies but for real. This group worked at night during World War II, patrolling gas storage tanks in the Los Angeles area, looking for saboteurs or any suspicious characters. In 1942 Jones was invited to Boston for a Victory Bond benefit drive where he lost his life (as did nearly four hundred others) in the tragic fire at the famous Coconut Grove nightclub.

For the great western movie classic *Red River*, starring John Wayne and Montgomery Clift, Bob Brown made

 *Bob's talents drew many to his studio. Here is a sketch for a leather mask he produced (to look like iron) for the motion picture the **Man in the Iron Mask** (1939).*

BOOTS FOR
BORIS KARLOFF
"AXMAN"
TOWER of LONDON
MOVIE MADE 1940

both men low-slung single holsters. The holster rigs Bob made for these two stars were completely different from anything Hollywood had seen previously. In addition, he made a pair of beautiful hand carved boots for Wayne.

So many things happened in Bob Brown's life in Hollywood that seemed unimportant at the time. One such incident occurred when a young man came into Bob's shop back in 1942 to have double taps put on his dancing shoes. This young man was Gene Kelly and he had just appeared on the Broadway. Gene tested the taps on Bob's floor with **Shuffle off to Buffalo**. About this same time Bob was asked to take the measurements of a little eight-year-old girl. The little girl: Shirley Temple. Bob put the first taps on the shoes of a sixteen-year-old Ann Miller. Then one day in 1947, a young radio announcer came into Bob's shop to have a single-holster belt created. This young man was Rex Allen.

On several occasions Basil Rathbone and Nigel Bruce came into Bob's shop just to watch him carve out another masterpiece. These two gentlemen, you may remember, as Sherlock Holmes and his sidekick Dr. Watson.

Bob Brown had many interesting and unusual people come into his shop on Hollywood Boulevard in

*Brown also designed and produced boots worn by Boris Karloff in the 1940 film **Tower of London**.*

Hollywood. Robert Bray came into Bob's shop because he saw a gun holster in the window that had his initials on it: B.B. Bob Brown or Bob Bray: same initials. The two became good friends over time and hunting partners for some twenty years. Bob Bray played the role of Corey Stewart, a forest ranger, in the TV series *Lassie*.

Bob Brown had a couple of rather unusual friends. One was "Carbine" Williams. David Marshall Williams was serving thirty years in Caladonia State prison in North Carolina. While imprisoned, he invented the M-1 carbine. President Franklin D. Roosevelt gave Williams a full pardon. And after his release, Williams traveled to Bob's shop, spending three months in the shop with Bob watching closely while Brown did his leatherwork. Bob made all the scabbards for all the guns Williams made while in prison. After Williams's death all of his arms and machinery were bequeathed to the State of North Carolina.

Hollywood made a movie about "Carbine Williams." MGM made the movie of the same name: *Carbine Williams*, which starred James Stewart. Al Jennings, a good friend of Bob's, had a .45 caliber Tommy gun — a machine gun that had been used in the famous Valentines Day Massacre (on Clark Street in Chicago in 1929). Ted

Bob loved to relax by taking time to ride.

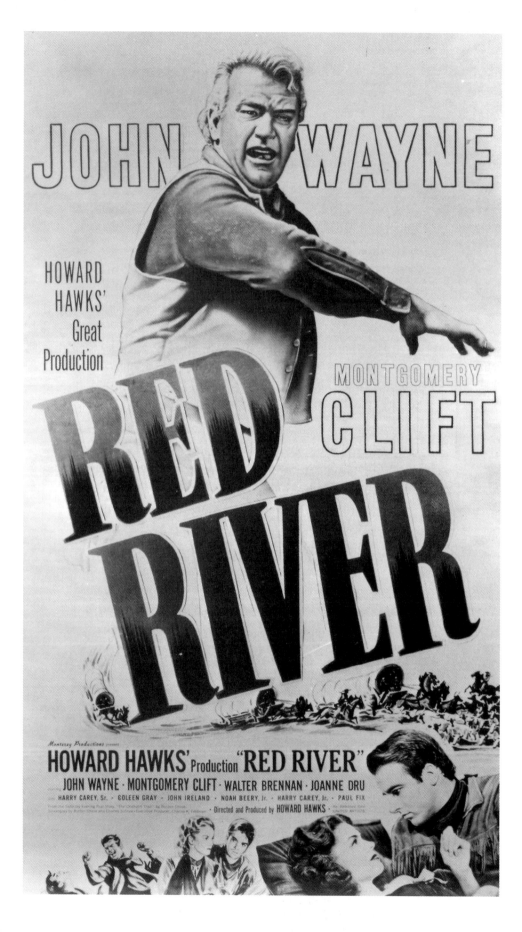

Newberry, one Al Capone's henchmen, had given the gun to Jennings. Al, in turn, gave the gun to Williams. Before this transaction was complete Bob Brown emptied the fifty-round clip and kept the .45 caliber shells that were not fired during the famous massacre in 1929.

Among Bob Brown's most unusual acquaintances, was the famous Oklahoma outlaw, Al Jennings. This short man (about 5'3") became very close to Bob over the years. They got along from the very first day they met. On their first visit Al told Bob a few stories of his escapades in Oklahoma and Texas.

Starting at the age of thirteen, Al Jennings carried a Colt .45 with a 4" barrel. The .45 first appeared in 1873. He killed his first man that same year. The incident occurred when Al was working as a cowboy for a cattle outfit. He was eating his breakfast one morning —a plate of bacon, beans, and biscuits. Al set his plate down on the ground for a second and the bully of the outfit came over and ground his boot into Al's plate. Al, having a short fuse, got so angry that he pulled his .45 and shot the guy on the spot.

Bob Brown, now of Big Bear City, California has several hours of extensive interviews on tape with his good friend.

John Wayne and Montgomery Clift were among the many who wore costumes and leather gear designed and produced by Bob Brown.

TEMPLE
...nt Pictures

According to his own testimony, Alphonso Jackson Jennings was born in Tazewell County, Virginia, on November 25, 1863. His father was born in the same county and his mother was born in Smyth County. Al's father was Judge J.D.F. Jennings, who practiced his profession in Comanche County, Kansas, before moving his family into Indian Territory in Tecumseh, Oklahoma Territory.

Regardless of the "comic-opera-bandit" brand that some historians have pinned on him, Al Jennings was clearly a gifted man. He was barely 20 years old when he graduated from the University of Virginia School of Law. He put out his shingle in Kansas, where his father was a judge. Shortly afterwards, he opened a law office in Oklahoma City, Oklahoma Territory, later moving on to El Reno, Canadian County where he went into partnership with his brother Ed.

In 1892, Al was elected county attorney of Canadian County. With Al moving up in the world, Ed formed a partnership with another brother, Frank. They opened an office in Woodard, Oklahoma Territory. Business prospered in this town that sheltered some of the most vicious outlaws in the West. Al brought many an outlaw to justice,

Even Shirley Temple had tap shoes produced by Bob Brown.

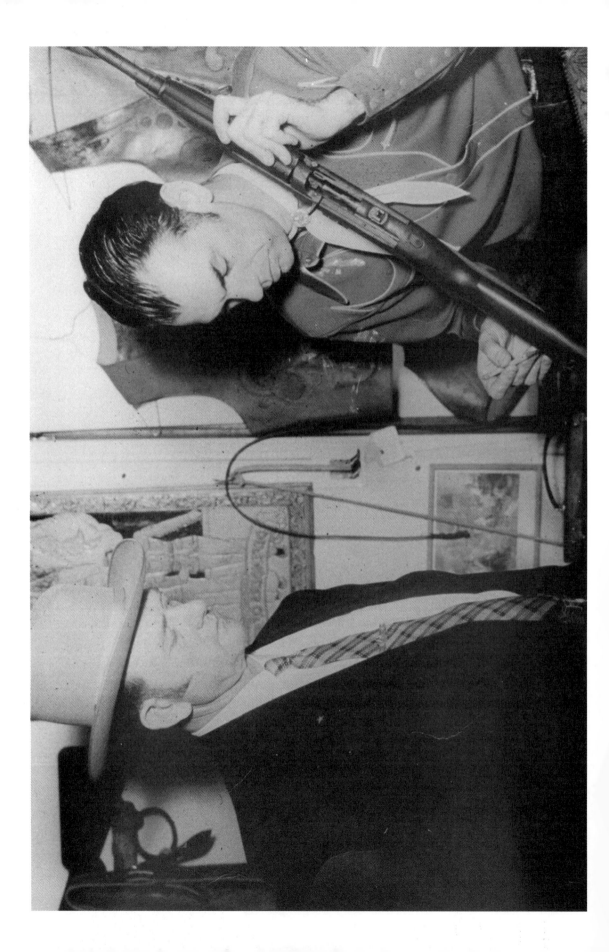

but failed to gain the nomination for a second term. After having served as Canadian County Attorney for two years, Al took a train to Woodard, to rejoin his brothers in their thriving law practice.

There lived in Woodard, a prominent attorney who was as fast with a gun as he was with his mouth. His name was Temple Houston — son of Sam Houston, liberator of the Republic of Texas. In Woodard, Houston, always seemed to get the best of Al Jennings in a courtroom. This caused considerable hard feelings on the part of the whole family, including Judge John Jennings, Al's father. Ed and John, brothers of Al, were the most vicious of the boys and had been in numerous gunfights. They had made some pretty strong threats against Houston, and he was aware of them.

About 10:30 A.M., one morning, Ed and John decided to stop in the Woodard Saloon to have a drink. Both boys were only being about 17 years old, but age didn't matter in those days. As long as you could do a man's work, you could drink with the men. As Ed and John entered the saloon they both spotted Temple Houston standing at the bar sipping a drink and talking with the bartender. After a few minutes they began to argue with Houston. After they

*David Marshall "Carbine" Williams meets with
Bob Brown at his Hollywood Boulevard shop.*

made several threats, Houston challenged the brothers to a fight. Ed said "Houston you know we don't stand a chance in a gunfight!" Being a dramatic type, Houston then ripped open his shirt with both hands and said, "Shoot. You haven't got the guts! You dirty bastards!" About this time, the youngest brother, John, who had moved over behind Ed, drew his gun and fired over Ed's shoulder. The shot missed Temple and he shot Ed between the eyes before he could empty his holster. As Ed fell dead (his gun still holstered), Temple shot John in the chest. Temple Houston then left the saloon and walked to his home about five blocks up the street from the saloon. No one dared to try and stop him.

During subsequent court proceedings, Houston was found innocent. Declining to remain in Woodard, Judge Jennings relocated to Tecumseh. It was alleged, and not surprisingly, that Temple Houston's self-defense plea and his subsequent release had embittered Frank and Al Jennings. The two brothers decided to find a new career. They would align themselves against the law and they both hit the hoot owl trail.

On a warm spring day in 1896 things began to happen. Five masked and armed men boarded a Santa Fe passen-

Brown with a new friend (soon-to-be long-term friend) famous outlaw Al Jennings.

ger train at Edmond, Oklahoma, when it stopped at a water-refueling tank. Intent on robbing the train, they were shocked to find no gold in the express car and no money in the safe. After fleecing the passengers of nearly $500 they mounted up and rode away at an ever-quickening tempo. The bandits were soon identified as Al and Frank Jennings, brothers Pat and Morris O'Malley, and Little Dick West.

With posses combing the territory for the gang. Al went to visit his father at Tecumseh, while the others rode hard to get to the home of Laurie Whipple in Pottawatomie County. Previously, another Whipple family had sheltered other outlaws: Bill Dalton, Doolin, and the Jennings band. The house provided a handy hidey-hole for outlaws on the dodge. Here they were safe. Mr. Whipple's wife, the former Eva Dalton, was the sister, of Grat, Bill, Bob, and Emmett Dalton.

Leaving his father's house Al Jennings set spurs to his chestnut pony and galloped toward the Whipple farm in a fury of dust. Shortly afterwards the Jennings gang swooped down on the MK&T train at Bond Switch, twenty-odd-miles south of Muskogee. But with cool nerve and lighting speed, the engineer plowed the train through

Bob went out of his way to have a cake made for Al's 90th birthday — a cake that Al didn't eat.

HARTSOOK PHOTO

cross ties piled on the tracks and out of harm's way. This was only an example of the unfortunate luck that would befall the Jennings gang.

The boys barely escaped with their lives when a posse came out of nowhere and thwarted their attempt to rob a train near Purcell. The bank in Minco looked as easy as eating pie, so Al sent Pat O'Malley into town to case the joint. Pat reported back that every path, trail and road into town was an armed camp with sheriff's deputies and marshals lined up like the king's soldiers on parade. No doubt the marshals and sheriffs had anticipated their shenanigans.

The outlaws seemed beaten. But not quite! Word of mouth reached the gang that Marshals Bud Ledbetter, Bill Tilghman and Chris Madsen were dogging their hoof beats, with reinforcements steadily coming. But nothing was so utterly discouraging that Al Jennings did not want to give it a try. He looked around and decided that a desolate point between Minco and Chickasha would be a good place to knock over a Rock Island train.

The next day all the newspapers reported how the robbers compelled a work gang foreman to flag down the train in

Al Jennings was graduate of the University of Virginia School of Law.

broad daylight. Subsequently, Conductor Dan Dacy found himself staring into a Colt .45 pistol. One of the gang took control of the engineer and fireman, while Al Jennings and Dick West raided the express car. When the express messenger convinced them he did not know the combination to the safe, they decided to use dynamite to blow open the two safes. The explosion shattered the safes and blew the train car to smithereens. Again they were forced to rob the passengers.

On one occasion, a newspaper editor received an anonymous letter in which the writer declared that he had recognized one of the bandits who had taken his money and his gold watch. His name, the author announced, was Al Jennings. Another piece of bad luck!

The Spike-S ranch was a ghostly looking place, half-light by a midnight moon on November 30, 1897. Famished, the two O'Malleys and Al Jennings stopped there for food and some oats for their weary horses. Little Dick West was not with them. The experiences he had lately with the Jennings gang convinced him to put spurs to his horse and go in a different direction.

The next morning Mrs. Harless (who owned the Spike-S) sent her brother to the barn to get some eggs. When her

Al opened a law office in Kansas where his father was a judge.

brother Dutch did not return she began to worry. Unknown to those inside the house, Bud Ledbetter and his posse had the house surrounded. When Dutch had entered the barn he was hogtied by the posse. Soon curiosity got the best of Mrs. Harless and she went to the barn. Ledbetter instructed her to tell the Jennings bunch to surrender or be shot down. She delivered the message then scooted out the door to safety. Al Jennings was fast becoming accustomed to being surrounded by posses. Suddenly there was the ripping sound of heavy-caliber bullets slamming into the house. Al's rifle jerked into action. A steady drumming of bullets sent Tolbert and Marshal Ledbetter ducking for cover. One of Al's slugs went through Tolbert's brand new sombrero. It was time to pull up stakes and get out of Dodge. Al gave the signal and the boys whirled out the back door like a hurricane. Jake Elliott was the only one in a position to see them fleeing. His long iron belched fire but soon they were out of his vision. Frank Jennings had twenty holes in his clothing and Al had taken a bullet just above his knee. Ledbetter later estimated that 100 bullets had peppered the house.

The gang made it through the night and the next morning they waylaid the driver of a spring-wagon. Al was

A closeup of a face that saw many events in the final days of the "Old West."

bleeding badly, so they headed for Sam Baker's place. Sam patched him up and gang lit out for Benny Price's ranch. Benny harbored them for a time, but they were not yet out of danger. Unknown to the gang, Sam Baker had no sooner waved good-bye than he saddled his mare and beat a path into town to warn deputy Marshal Ledbetter that the Jennings gang was in the vicinity. Hoping for a reward, Sam agreed to lead Al and his gang into an ambush.

Sam placed the gang in a wagon and covered them with hay. Under narrow shafts of moonlight, he took the hardened outlaws across a dirt road by a creek and departed, saying he had to return home. Frank Jennings then took the reigns and headed into the solitude, unbroken say for the heartbeats of the men in the posse waiting in a cluster of shrubs by the creek. A jerk of the wagon told the outlaws, hiding in the wagon under the hay, that something was wrong. When Al lifted his head up, he was peering into Ledbetter's rifle. There was no chance of escape this time.

The Jennings gang was transported by train to Muskogee, where Al, Frank, and the O'Malley brothers were thrown

Temple Houston, son of Texas hero Sam Houston, was a lawyer in the Oklahoma Territory. It was he who killed Al Jenning's brother in a gunfight in Woodward, OK — an event that led to Al's life on the run.

into a jail cell. Five months later, former gang member, Little Dick West was gunned down by federal officers on April 7, 1898 five miles outside of Guthrie.

The Cruce Brothers defended Al Jennings, free of charge (pro bono), in court as a favor to Al's father. Al took the stand and blamed his outlaw career on the death of his brother. The jury didn't care about Al's feelings. He was convicted and sentenced to twenty-five years in Leavenworth. Before the sentenced started, Al, Frank, and the O'Malley brothers were indicted for robbing the United States mails. Al's trial was first. Found guilty, he was sentenced to life in the Federal prison at Columbus, Ohio.

When Frank and The O'Malley brothers were slated for trial, they agreed to plea bargain with Judge Townsend and the U.S. Attorney. If Al's sentence was commuted to five years, they would plead guilty and accept the same sentence, thus saving the state a long and expensive trial. The terms were accepted. President William McKinley commuted Al's life sentence to five years. He served his time and eventually returned to Oklahoma.

As luck would have it — bad luck in Al's case — Federal officers were waiting for him upon his return so that they

Deputy U.S. marshal, Bud Ledbetter assisted in the capture of the Jennings Gang in 1897.

could escort Al to Leavenworth prison to serve his five-year sentence. In less than four years he was back in Chickasha, a free man, pardoned by President Theodore Roosevelt. Chris Maden gave Al enough money to take a train to Lawton, where one of Al's brothers lived. Frank Jennings and the O'Malley boys served their time and returned to Oklahoma, leading respectable and useful lives.

In Lawton, Al set up a law practice and in 1914 he filed papers to run for Governor of Oklahoma. The newspaper headlines read on January 19, 1914: "EX-BANDIT SEEKS TO BE GOVERNOR." In one story, Al Jennings told why he wanted to "rule" Oklahoma: "I'm entering the race," Jennings reporters in New York, "as a Democrat. Many of my friends have urged me to seek an independent nomination, but I have always been a Democrat. My objective is to clean up the party in Oklahoma. I intend to fight double-dealing, political thieves, with whom no self-respecting outlaw of former years can associate. All I want is to see absolutely honest men at the head of the government and after I have announced my candidacy, if some man whose integrity and uprightness are unquestioned becomes a candidate I shall withdraw and support him with all my ability." In the

Al Jennings displaying his pardon from President Theodore Roosevelt.

AL JENNINGS, THE OUTLAW WHO RAN FOR GOVERNOR OF OKLAHOMA

by Bill Kelly

The Monmouth, Illinois Daily Review, dated January 19, 1914, bannered: "EX-BANDIT SEEKS TO BE GOVERNOR: Al Jennings Tells Why He Wants to Rule Oklahoma."

The article stated his platform:

"I am entering the race," said Mr. Jennings in New York recently, "as a Democrat. Many of my friends have urged me to seek an independent nomination, but I have always been a Democrat. My object is to clean up the party in Oklahoma. I intend to fight double dealing, political thieves, with whom no self-respecting outlaw of former years can associate.

democratic primary, Al Jennings lost out to Supreme Court Justice Robert L. Williams by a vote of 21,732 to 33,605. Williams went on to win the general election by a vote of 100,904 to 95,904, defeating his Republican opponent.

When Al Jennings and William Sidney Porter — better known as the writer O'Henry — got out of the state penitentiary, they robbed banks, stage coaches and anything else that came to their minds. Porter held the horses and Al did the dirty work. Porter was always the lookout. Al later gifted his friend Bob Brown with a Wells Fargo moneybag that he and O'Henry lifted off a stage in Muskogee Indian Territory. In that bag, Al had stored nearly one hundred live .45 automatic shells taken from one of the Tommy-guns used in the St. Valentines Day Massacre of 1929 and mentioned earlier in this story.

After failing in his bid to become the governor of Oklahoma Al got married and moved out of Oklahoma to Tarzana, California. The year was 1916. Soon afterward, Al opened his own motion picture studio and made short (two and three-reelers) westerns. He wrote all his own stories from the real-life experiences of O'Henry and himself. After his movie career was over he lived out the rest of his life with his wife, Maud, in Tarzana.

The former outlaw ran for governor of Oklahoma.

Bob Brown first met Al Jennings in 1940 when Tex Cooper, a western extra, introduced them. Tex brought Al to Bob's shop at 5910 Hollywood Boulevard. Al and Bob hit it off at their first meeting. Over time, Al would bring Bob eggs from his home in Tarzana — usually two-dozen eggs at a time. In this way Bob could help Al make a few bucks. Al was living on a state pension and times were tough. He and Maud were very poor by any standard. Bob made Al a waist belt that pleased Al so much that he brought Bob his holster and single-action Colt .45 which Bob displayed for all to see in his shop window.

Bob use to set in his swivel chair in the window of his shop and look up the hills and see the white letters of the "Hollywood Land" sign. This was in 1938 and soon after the wind blew down the "Land" part of the sign. The sign, originally intended as a real estate promotion, was never repaired and the letters for "Land" were not replaced. The sign has since become, perhaps the single-most famous of all Hollywood landmarks.

Al Jennings may have had some bad luck with attempting to rob trains, but he had good luck in picking friends like Bob Brown — better known as Bob Brown of Hollywood "The Michelangelo of Leather." In November of 1961 Al

Photograph in LA Times (March 10, 1957) showing Actor Hugh O'Brien (TV's Wyatt Earp) with Jennings who knew the real Earp and thought he was 'a skunk.'

Jennings' wife, Maud died at home. Al took to his bed, and there, on December 26, the day after Christmas 1961, passed away at the age of ninety-eight. With the death of Al Jennings, the only train and bank robber to run for governor of Oklahoma (let alone any state or territory) passed into history.

Bob Brown relaxing in the 1950's — the artist who designed the logo for Max Factor, made gloves for Tyrone Power, and silver-studded dog collars for Cole Porter.

CHAPTER 10

THOSE OTHER SILVER-SCREEN HEROS

MONTE HALE
(1921-)

REPUBLIC STUDIOS' FIRST WESTERN produced in color was *Home on the Range*, featuring a new cowboy star: Monte Hale. The movie was released in 1946. Monte Hale played his guitar, rode and sang his way through nineteen feature films before he took off his spurs and hung up his guns and put his horse Pardner out to pasture. This young handsome singing cowboy was

playing small town Texas honkytonks when he came to the attention of a renowned Hollywood producer. Quickly signed to a Republic Studio contract, Monte shot to the top of the western charts, winning over the ladies with his charming smile and the gents with his rough-and-tumble antics. Following his nineteen-picture career with Republic, Monte eventually returned to his first love, singing. You know, many of us remember Monte Hale as the sweetest-singing, rip-roaring cowboy this side of the Panhandle! Standard biographical stats list Monte's birthday as June 8, 1921 and his birthplace as San Angelo, TX — although some sources argue that he was born in 1919, and Monte supposedly told a film festival crowd in Memphis that he had been born in Ada, OK, rather than Texas. Texas just sounded better for publicity purposes he told the gathering. He appeared in the 1956 box-office smash, *Giant*.

REX ALLEN (1922-1999)

Return with me to the days when the west was really wild and ride with the sharpest-shooting and one of the best singing cowboys to ever hit the high plains. Saddled up on his famous steed Koko, "the Miracle Horse," sat singing cowboy Rex Allen — already topping the Country-Western charts, when in 1949, he was tapped by Republic Studios to star in a series of sagebrush adventures. His famous voice (that voice enabled him to narrate more than eighty Disney films in later years) and matinee idol looks helped Allen become a screen sensation virtually overnight. His first Republic movie made him one of the top five western box-office draws; it was entitled The Arizona Cowboy. Allen, forever known as "The Arizona Cowboy," went on to headline in thirty-four more features for Republic before he found lasting fame on television (he starred in his own series, **Frontier Doctor**). Koko, by the way, appeared for the first time in Allen's second film, **The Hills of Oklahoma**. Gene Autry said of Rex Allen: "He came along too late. Good thing for Roy and me. He could out sing either one of us, could fight better than both of us put together, and he sure was better looking than Roy or me!" Rex had what many thought was the most beautiful horse in the movies. Koko was a stud that did most of the same tricks as Trigger, largely because the same man — Glen Randall, trained him. Koko, the personal horse of Allen, was half Morgan and half Quarter horse. He carried Allen through one hundred-and-ninety-eight Westerns and many personal appearances. Many

P-1872-11

will remember Rex's deep voice on such recordings as *Streets of Laredo* and *Crying in the Chapel*. The world was saddened to learn of the death of this singer-actor on December 18, 1999 in a bizarre accident in which his caretaker ran him over with a car. In an interview completed a little over a year before his death, Allen said: "Wanna see the American dream? You're looking at it."

DON "RED" BARRY
(1912-1980)

Don Barry, born Donald Barry De Acosta on January 11, 1912, was struggling as a bit player when his career really got a big boost. He was given his first starring role, which earned him a nickname "Red" that he'd carry for the rest of his life. A former college football star, he got his early acting experience on the stage. He eventually played heavies for a number of Hollywood studios before his big break came. Don starred in the 1940 Republic Studio's serial *The Adventures of Red Ryder*. He would then forever be known as Don "Red" Barry. He played the part very well and was well liked by fans. From 1942 through 1945 Don was voted one of the top-ten moneymakers in

997-C

western films. Don was born and raised in a very poor section of Houston, TX. Playing football in high school, Don took All-State honors. His team went to California to play an All-Southern California team. It was there that he met John Wayne and Mickey Rooney. After the game, the two told Don if he ever came back that way to look them up. They promised that they would help him, if he wanted to try and get into the movies. And that's what he did. The first movie Don appeared in was with John Wayne in *Wyoming Outlaw*. In addition to the Red Ryder role, he also portrayed other characters such as the Tulsa Kid and the Cyclone Kid. His career ended for the most part in 1950, although he appeared in supporting roles in small, inexpensive films into the 1970's. He committed suicide on July 17, 1980 in Hollywood.

SUNSET CARSON
(1920-1990)

The baby-faced action ace of the silver screen, Sunset Carson, was born in Plainview, Texas (some sources give Gracemont, OK) with the name Mickey Harrison (some sources state Winifred Maurice Harrison) on November

12, 1920. Republic Studios changed it to Sunset Carson. Sunset competed in rodeos as a youngster. And the rodeo circuit proved to be beneficial after he winged his way to the Hollywood sound stages began thrilling audiences on Saturday afternoons with his honest-to-goodness riding, roping, and shooting. Smiley Burnette was available for a new series due to Gene Autry's enlistment in the military. Republic signed Smiley to the Carson series and strangely enough, gave the sidekick top billing over the youthful actor. Sunset Carson was another one of those cowboys that had a beautiful horse. Tall and handsome, and generally clad in black, Sunset was a dashing figure on his snow-white horse Cactus. When Sunset first acquired the horse, its name was Silver, but because of the popularity of the Lone Ranger's horse of the same name, it was necessary for Sunset to change his horse's name. And so it became Cactus. Carson left us on May 1, 1990 in Reno, NV.

THE THREE MESQUITEERS RAY "CRASH" CORRIGAN (1902-1976)

When the script needed a daredevil with athletic ability, Ray filled the order completely. Ray was truly a daredevil and considered the feats he performed merely a part of his daily routine. Ray "Crash" Corrigan (born Raymond Bernard on February 14, 1902 in Milwaukee, WI) appeared in twenty-four episodes of the poplar Republic Studios series *The Three Mesquiteers*, portraying the character called "Tucson Smith." He later starred in the *Range Busters* series. Although a star athlete in his youth, Ray suffered from curvature of the spine. Bernard McFadden of Hollywood helped restore Ray's back to proper order through physical therapy at the McFadden Studio. While in therapy the director of the silent Tarzan films discovered Ray, and he soon found himself swinging on vines for Johnny Weismuller — which earned him his nickname "Crash" due to the fact that he would do any stunt they asked him to attempt. Ray retired from movies in 1944 to concentrate on his own business —

Corriganville, an authentic western town that was frequently used as a movie set. "Crash" died in Brookings Hollow, Oregon of a heart attack in 1976.

THE THREE MESQUITEERS
MAX TERHUNE
(1891-1973)

A master when it came to showmanship, Max Terhune (born February 12, 1891 in Franklin, IN) entertained hundreds of thousands over the years with his feats of magic, ventriloquism, impersonations, and comedy. It was Gene Autry who brought Max to Hollywood in the first place. Terhune's movie career began in 1936 when he appeared with Autry in the movie *Ride Ranger Ride*. Later he rode with the best when he became the third member of *The Three Mesquiteers*. He made twenty-four films in this excellent series and made a friend for life in co-star Ray Corrigan. After these features were completed, Max again joined up with friend Ray in a new western series called *The Range Busters* produced by Monogram

between 1940 and 1944. Through both series Max used a ventriloquist's dummy named Elmer — a first in westerns. He was a big hit with both the young and older moviegoers alike. The roles gave Max Terhune a chance to show off one of his talents as a ventriloquist — and Max was one of the best. Max starred in a series with John Wayne and also a few movies with Johnny Mack Brown. Max died following complications from a heart attack and stroke on June 5, 1973.

THE THREE MESQUITEERS
ROBERT LIVINGSTONE
(1904-1988)

Prior to becoming a cowboy star, Bob (who was born Robert Edgar Randall on December 9, 1904 in Quincy, IL) worked as a seaman, lumberjack, a ranch hand, and even as a reporter for a Los Angeles newspaper Bob moved to California when he was twelve years old and began working in films in 1929. Perhaps Robert

Livingston's most memorable role, besides being a member of **The Three Mesquiteers** (in which he made twenty-nine appearances), was his role as the Lone Ranger in the Republic Serial **The Lone Ranger Rides Again**. Livingston was the brother to movie singing-cowboy star Jack (Addison) Randall who died suddenly while filming at the Iverson Ranch location in 1945. Many people remember Bob Livingston as "Stony Brooke" the handsome, dashing Mesquiteer who had a quick wit, a fast gun, and a sharp eye for the ladies. Livingston died on March 7, 1988 in Tarzana, CA.

BUSTER CRABBE
(1909-1983)

Buster Crabbe was born on February 7, 1909 in Oakland, California. His real name was Clarence Linden Crabbe. His first claim to fame came as an Olympic Bronze-medal-winner in swimming in the 1928 games. In 1932 Buster set a world record in the 400-meter event at the Olympic games, breaking Johnny Weissmuler's (the future Tarzan) record. He won a gold medal and would

eventually hold sixteen swimming records. Crabbe auditioned and passed a Hollywood screen test and was subsequently cast in westerns. His first western was ***Man From the Forest*** shot at Paramount with Randolph Scott. He would appear in two more Randolph Scott films before taking over the ***Zane Grey*** series for Paramount. His greatest fame came in the ***Flash Gordon*** movie serial and his TV role as ***Captain Gallant of the Foreign Legion***. Buster had a great sidekick in Al "Fuzzy" St. John. He made thirty-six B-westerns with Fuzzy between 1941 and 1946. Buster Crabbe, "King of the Wild West," passed away April 23, 1983 in Scottsdale, Arizona.

EDDIE DEAN
(1907-1999)

Edgar Dean Glosup (born July 9, 1907 in Posey, TX), known to his fans as Eddie Dean, had a great singing voice. That voice and his likable personality took him to the lights of movie sound stages where he became a top-money-making western star. Over the years, he made a lot of Saturday afternoons enjoyable for thousands of fans playing his guitar, sitting astride his horse Flash. Dean has

been credited for writing over one hundred songs including the hit, ***Hillbilly Heaven***. One Eddie Dean western (a PRC production entitled ***Song of Old Wyoming***) introduced Lash LaRue who would ride on to become a cowboy star in his own right. Before becoming a star, Eddie would appear in many of the better cowboy films with the likes of Roy Rogers, Gene Autry, and Hopalong Cassidy. He made nine Hoppy films and sang in most of them. He eventually got to play white-hat roles as well. I've heard it said that back in 1986 at the Western Film Fair in Charlotte, NC, there was quite an Eddie Dean night to remember. Fans recall that he brought down the house with his guitar and song in a performance that was simply tremendous. Following complications of lung disease, Dean passed away on March 4, 1999 in Thousands Oaks, CA.

TRT-49

TIM HOLT
(1918-1973)

Tim Holt (born Charles John Holt, III on February 5, 1918 in Beverly Hills, CA) was inducted into the Cowboy Hall of Fame after having a highly successful career in B-Western movies. Tim had a great sidekick in "Chito Jose Gonzales Bustomino Rafferty" —whose real name was Richard Martin. He and Tim were good friends both on and off the screen. Tim Holt was a top-notch cowboy star for RKO Pictures where he earned the prestige of being a top-money-making western star. Tim's father was Jack Holt the former silent-screen star who had successfully made the move to sound and continued as a character actor late in his career. Tim also had a sister who appeared frequently in movies — Jennifer Holt who was one gorgeous beautiful lady. I first saw her in *Stick to Your Guns* (a Hopalong Cassidy film) and Brad King was singing to her. Tim had only toiled for a little over a year on the RKO back lots before the studio offered him a chance to star in his own western series. When George O'Brien re-entered the Navy during World War II, his departure set the stage for Tim's future as a cowboy star. Holt died in Shawnee, OK on February 15, 1973 following a bout with cancer.

BUCK JONES
(1891-1942)

Buck Jones was born Charles Frederick Gebhart in Vincennes, Indiana in 1891. Buck Jones rose to become one of America's best-known motion picture cowboy stars. Jones had been starring in the ***Rough Riders*** series and had just signed a new contract with Monogram Pictures at the time of his untimely death. Many will recall that Jones, along with more than four hundred others died when the Coconut Grove, a Boston nightclub exploded in flame in 1942. Buck Jones was hurt several times in the making of his westerns: he broke a foot, broke both hands and both collarbones. He was nearly roasted alive in another film. That particular film had one scene that called for him to be soaked with gasoline and set on fire. The fire spread too fast and Buck started to run, requiring someone to punch him out after which he was wrapped him in a blanket to smother the fire. The last western series Buck Jones starred in was the ***Rough Rider*** series with Tim McCoy and Raymond Hatton.

LASH LARUE
(1917-1999)

Lash LaRue, dressed in black and cracking a whip, cut a figure that few who ever saw him in action can forget. Born Alfred LaRue in Gretna, LA on June 15, 1917, he moved to California as a teen and got the acting bug while attending college. He obtained a screen test at Warner Brothers at the urging of actor George Brent. Lash LaRue's western career began in 1945 with Song of Old Wyoming, an Eddie Dean film. He was an instant hit and signed quickly for more films. Success then led to his own series in 1947 at PRC. His black outfit, whip and beautiful stallion Black Diamond made quite an impression on young audiences. His films were a great success at the box office and he soon became a star. It wasn't long before his character in films simply became "Lash." In the beginning, he was the Cheyenne Kid or Marshall Davis, but by any name he was the man in black with the bullwhip. His series was very profitable which allowed Lash to tour the South almost constantly with his stage show. These appearances made him even more popular with young moviegoers who surely believed he was "The King of the Bullwhip." The B-western hero was married and divorced ten time — a record for any Hollywood western actor. His last appearances were in 1990: a movie, *Escape* and a TV movie with Kris Kristofferson and Willie Nelson entitled *Pair of Aces*. He died on May 21, 1999 in Burbank, CA.

TIM MCCOY
(1891-1978)

One of the best-known cowboys of the 1930's was Tim McCoy. Known as "Colonel Tim" to millions of fans and moviegoers, McCoy appeared in rodeos and Wild West shows all over the country for many years following the end of his screen career. He always projected a good clean cowboy image to his fans. Born on April 10, 1891 in Saginaw, MI, Tim actually lived in the "real west" and was a devotee of Indian culture history and language. After leaving St. Ignatius College (Chicago) he settled in Wyoming and actually homesteaded 5,700 acres where he raised horses. This cowboy was "The Real McCoy" and gained the rank of Colonel for his long years of Army service (having served in

World War I and Adjutant General of Wyoming until 1921). After his stint with the military, he served as territorial Indian agent in Wyoming while he ranched. Those connections with local Indians enabled him to provide Jessie Lasky of Famous Players with hundreds of extras for Hollywood films. In 1922 he served as a technical director for *The Covered Wagon* and eventually became the only B-western star for MGM Studios. Signing with Universal in 1930 Tim made the first all-talking serial, *The Indians Are Coming*. Tim eventually joined Columbia's roster of stars and was supported in his first two films by a very young John Wayne. In 1935 he departed from films to tour with the Ringling Brothers Circus and then his own Wild West show. In 1940 he returned to Hollywood to work with Buck Jones and Raymond Hatton. The sudden death of Jones and World War II saw McCoy return to the Army (Air Corps). He made a few films after the end of the war and did some television work. His second wife, Inga Arvad died in 1973. A year later he was inducted into the Cowboy Hall of Fame. As a young man he personally knew Wyatt Earp, Bat Masterson, and Bill Hickok. Tim McCoy died of a heart attack at age eighty-six in Nogales, AZ on January 28, 1978.

KEN MAYNARD
(1895-1973)

Ken Maynard, riding his horse Tarzan may have been the best horseback rider that ever appeared in B-Western movies. Ken Maynard and Tarzan were one of the great cowboy-and-wonder-horse teams to hit the western screen. This six-footer was a rodeo cowboy long before movie fame came his way, getting his start as a trick rider with the Buffalo Bill Wild West Show. He won the National Trick Riding title in 1920 and 1923, while performing with the Ringling Brothers Circus. His screen debut was in 1923 in *The Man Who Won* and he retired in 1944 after making his last film entitled Harmony Trail. Publicity releases from the studios incorrectly listed Ken's birthplace as Mission, TX, when in reality he was born in Vevay, IN on July 21, 1895. Maynard displayed daring skills in every film in which he appeared. It is to his credit that he was the first movie cowboy to feature western music in his early sound pictures. This giant cowboy star's movie career spanned more than twenty years. Super cowboy star Gene Autry made his debut in a Ken Maynard film: *In Old Santa Fe*. When Ken went on one of his well-known ego rampages at Mascot Studios just prior to beginning a new

Ken Maynard - 14

serial, Nat Levine fired him and took a chance on a young cowboy singer named Gene Autry. The rest of course is history! Western fans lost another cinema hero when Ken Maynard died in Woodland Hills, CA on March 23, 1973; he is buried at Forest Lawn Cypress near Los Angeles.

TOM MIX
(1880-1940)

Tom Mix, "King of the Cowboys" and Tony, "The Wonder Horse" are considered by many to be the best cowboy-horse teams ever seen in motion pictures. Tom Mix was the American hero-showman to millions of fans in silent films with Selig Shorts and Fox oater features through the late 1920's. Born in Mix Run, PA on January 6, 1880, his given name was Thomas Hezikiah Mix. The son of a lumberman, Tom was a one-time artillery sergeant, drum major, bartender, and sheriff-marshal. He appeared in a number of Wild West shows in the early 1900's, along with his wife Olive his first of five wives). Before actually getting in front

of a motion picture camera, Tom supplied Selig studios with cowboys and Indians as extras; in 1910 he provided horses and became a studio handler. His made his first movie in 1910 entitled ***Ranch Life in the Great Southwest***. During the early 1930's, Tom mainlined nine Universal westerns that included the superior and highly praised ***The Rider of Death Valley***. Tom Mix would close out his film career with Mascot Pictures — doing a fifteen-chapter serial entitled ***The Miracle Rider*** in 1935. Much of the material concerning Tom Mix's life and career, his birthplace, family ancestry, and alleged heroics were based on myth and fiction precipitated by early publicists of the time. When Mix first entered the movie industry and became Hollywood's first and foremost celluloid "King of the Cowboys," the studio felt the need to make more of him than was real. Tom was a professional showman through-and-through. It was age and injury that finally caught up with him. In ***The Miracle Rider*** some close-up scenes reveal just how true this was and that he was a bit slower and tired than in previous film. Sound was not friendly to Mix and he finally dropped out of the business, going on tour with the Sells Floto Circus and his own Tom Mix Circus. The world lost this favorite to an auto accident on October 12, 1940 in Florence, AZ.

1114-6

BOB STEELE
(1907-1988)

Born January 23, 1907 in Pendleton, Oregon, Bob Steele (born Robert Adrian Bradbury) was the epitome of a hard riding, fast riding, and quick drawing cowboy film hero. Bob was a boyhood friend of John Wayne and his dad was Robert N. Bradbury a Hollywood director. His first roles were as juveniles in silent films, such as *The Adventures of Bob and Bill*. He had more than 150 starring action packed films to his credit, among them sixteen of *The Three Mesquiteers* films for Republic. He also did *The Trailblazer* series for Monogram. At Republic he worked all over the lot — even playing Sunset Carson's younger brother in *Rio Grande Raiders* in 1946. After the Hollywood movie cowboy days, Steele went into television where he gained popularity as trooper Duffy on F-Troop. Unfortunately, unlike most of the B-western cowboy stars, Bob Steele was a very private person, and his fans are left with a large gap regarding his private life. Even little information is available regarding Steele's father, Robert North Bradbury, Sr., who directed many of the early westerns, including several in which Bob starred. Bob had a twin brother named Bill. Bob Steele will always be remembered by his fans as "Battling Bob." Steele died on December 21, 1988 in St. Joseph's Hospital in Burbank, CA after a lengthy illness.

WHIP WILSON
(1911-1964)

Whip Wilson or Roland Charles Meyers, his real name, was born June 16, 1911 in Granite City, Illinois. Whip Wilson's skill with a bullwhip led him to a movie contract with Monogram Studios where he became a western movie hero. Whip's sidekick was the grizzly-faced Andy Clyde (who earlier was sidekick to Hopalong Cassidy). Whip Wilson became memorable as the celluloid Range Rider on his white stallion Silver Bullet. The first film in that series was Canyon Raiders in 1951. Whip Wilson had a resemblance to Buck Jones, carried a whip like Lash LaRue, was given a Hollywood buildup like Roy Rogers, was given a hat by Mrs. Tom Mix, and was presented with a gun belt that had once

Whip W

belonged to Buck Jones. One would think with all these ingredients that a super star was in the making — but it was not to be. Wilson did gain some measure of fame by starring in twenty-two B-Western features, but after Andy Clyde left the series and Fuzzy Knight was brought in to replace him, the series went down hill. This, however, was not altogether Knight's fault.

JIMMY WAKELY
(1914-1982)

Jimmy Wakely was born James Clarence Wakely on February 16, 1914 in Mineola, Arkansas. Jimmy backed-up almost all the western stars during the 1940's, such as appearing in two *Hopalong Cassidy* films in 1941. He finally became a star in his own right in 1944 at Monogram Studios in *Song of the Range* with Dennis Moore and Lee "Lasse"" White as his co-stars. In 1936 Jimmy had his first real singing job at KTOK in Oklahoma at a fantastic salary of $8.50 a week. In 1937 he pitched patent medicine on the radio for $14.00 weekly. Teaming with Johnny Bond, Wakely began to perform locally and once backed-up Gene Autry when he appeared

on tour. Gene eventually put them on his national radio show. Jimmy made appearances in the ***Johnny Mack Brown-Tex Ritter*** series at Universal Studios. Jimmy worked at Universal, and later at Columbia, before his popularity as a singer got him his contract at Monogram in 1944. Jimmy Wakely would work in films through 1949 making thirty feature westerns. Jimmy had that youthful appeal and boyish charm. Plus, he possessed one of the best singing voices to ever grace the B-Western screens. We lost Jimmy Wakely on September 23, 1982 when he died of heart failure while living in California, the same year his wife Inez died. He is survived by four children.

CHAPTER 11

QUEENS OF THE SILVER-SCREEN

JENNIFER HOLT · ANNE GWYNNE
LOIS HALL · LINDA STIRLING
VIRGINIA MAYO · ELAINE RILEY
JUNE STORY · NELL O'DAY
PEGGY STEWART · ANNE JEFFREYS

JENNIFER HOLT
(1920- 1997)

JENNIFER HOLT (BORN ELIZABETH MARSHALL HOLT on November 10, 1920 in Hollywood) was in my opinion, the single-most beautiful, gorgeous saddle-gal to ever ride a pony. She was a refreshing, yet sophisticated lady. I loved her the first time I saw her and I've loved her ever since. Darling it's been a long time, but it seems like only yesterday when I saw her in *Stick To Your Guns* and Brad King was singing to her under the bright stars by an open campfire (that lucky guy). Jennifer was a leading lady at Universal Studios and at PRC to such popular B-Western cowboy stars as Johnny Mack Brown, Tex Ritter, Eddie Dean, and Lash LaRue. Jennifer Holt was a star in westerns of the 1940's. She was the daughter of Jack Holt, and the sister of Tim Holt. Her credits include such movies *Deep in the Heart of Texas*, *Gun Smoke*, *Under Western Skies*, and *Moon Over Montana*. Jennifer played opposite some of the great western stars including Rod Cameron, yet she was never entirely satisfied with the role of the western heroine. She died of cancer on November 21, 1997 in Dorset, England.

ANNE GWYNNE
(1918-)

Once signed by Universal Studios in 1939, Anne Gwynne (who was born Marguerite Gwynne Trice on December 10, 1918 in Waco, TX) immediately was thrust into well-received gallopers and musicals with stars like Johnny Mack Brown, Richard Arlen, and Abbott and Costello. Gwynne later appeared in the well-produced Rod Cameron A-Western Panhandle for United Artists (1948). Anne also did one picture at Columbia with Gene Autry in 1950. Born in San Antonio, TX on December 10, 1918, she moved with her parents in 1936 to Missouri where she attended Stevens College. In 1939 her father was transferred to Los Angeles. She moved joined her parents and immediately obtained modeling. She was approached by two studios but interviewed first with Universal. Anne's first western was *Oklahoma Frontier* (1939), a Johnny Mack Brown film. In 1940 she worked with Johnny again in *Bad Man from Red Butte*. Johnny Mack Brown just happened to be one of Anne Gwynne's childhood idols.

is Hall

LOIS HALL (1926-)

Lois Hall, born Lois Willows, was another of the B-Western beauties. She was born in Grand Rapids, Michigan August 22, 1926, but was raised in Pengilly, Minnesota. Her family moved to California in the 1930's for economic and health reasons: the Depression and her mother's arthritis. After high school graduation Lois attended the Pasadena Playhouse where she was spotted and signed by agent Gus Dembling. Lois didn't have a car and usually went on auditions and interviews by bus. Gus would meet her at the bus line and see to it that she got onto the studio sets. They worked together for seven years, until Gus' death. In her first serial, the 1949 *Adventures of Sir Galahad* shot at Columbia, Lois was the Lady of the Lake and George Reeves (later TV's Superman) played Sir Galahad. Lois started shooting westerns in 1949, including three with Johnny Mack Brown. She made two westerns with Whip Wilson: *Cherokee Uprising* in 1950 and *Night Raiders* in 1952. Lois also supported Charles Starrett and worked on *The Cisco Kid* TV show. In 1952 Lois had the opportunity to work with Jock Mahoney on his *Range Rider* series which was filmed by Gene Autry's Flying-A Productions. Lois was one of the classiest ladies to star in B-Westerns.

LINDA STIRLING (1921-1997)

She made her living getting beat up, tied up, gagged, and thrown off a horse. Linda Stirling was the last of the great "Serial Queens." She appeared in six Republic cliffhangers — the last in 1946. The native Californian (who was born Linda Schultz in Long Beach on October 21, 1921) started drama lessons at twelve and graduated from high school at the age of sixteen. A modeling career led her to Republic and into the title role in *The Tiger Woman* serial in 1944. She was not the outdoors type and could not ride, but she was a great looker and Republic needed someone right away for *The Tiger Woman*. Since she had to work on a serial for a month or more, westerns seemed like a vacation by comparison. During her career she would work with some of the greats in westerns — stars like Bill Elliott, Allen "Rocky" Lane, John Wayne, Sunset Carson, and Clayton Moore. Linda's favorite western was one with Sunset Carson entitled *Santa Fe Saddlemates* in 1945. Linda was married to screenwriter Sloan Nibley until his death in 1990. Nibley wrote most of the great Roy Rogers Republic westerns in the late 1940's, before turning to TV in the early 50's. Linda Stirling died of cancer on July 20, 1997 in Studio City, CA.

VIRGINIA MAYO
(1920-   )

This beautiful blonde actress was born Virginia Clara Jones on November 30, 1920 in St. Louis, Missouri and studied at her aunt's local drama school. She began her career as a dancer in vaudeville and in musical comedies before hitting Broadway. After appearing on Broadway in *Banjo Eyes*, an Eddie Cantor musical, and at Billy Rose's Diamond Horseshoe Club, she was spotted by Samuel Goldwyn and lured to Hollywood. In 1949 she was teamed with Joel McCrea in her first western Colorado Territory. The film established Mayo as an outdoor heroine — just right for epic westerns. Other western films included *Along the Great Divide* with Kirk Douglas, *The Iron Mistress* with Alan Ladd, Devil's Canyon with Dale Robertson, *The Proud Ones* with Robert Ryan, *The Tall Stranger* with McCrea, *The Big Land* with Alan Ladd, *Fort Dobbs* with Clint Walker, and the 1959 *Westbound* with "what-ever-happened-to" Randolph Scott.

ELAINE RILEY
(1923-   )

This lovely little lady, born in East Liverpool, England in 1923, was married to Richard Martin (Tim Holt's sidekick). She was born in Ohio and grew up in Manhattan in New York City. Her movie career began as a starlet at RKO Studios. She was placed in many pictures with only minor parts. Finally she was loaned out to do her first lead in a picture, which was a western, with "Hoppy" (William Boyd) and went on to star in five more of the Hopalong Cassidy films. William Boyd was a polished gentleman, a real professional, and was always a pleasant, warm and intelligent man. That is how Elaine Riley described William Boyd. In 1950 she starred along with her husband in Tim Holt's *Rider From Tucson*. She would also get to star in one western with Allan "Rocky" Lane, *Leadville Gunslinger* in 1952 for Republic Studios. Elaine said, in her own words, that working in westerns was "just pure fun." She appeared in other westerns with "Jocko" Mahoney as the *Range Rider*, Gene Autry, and some *Lone Ranger* episodes with Clayton Moore.

JUNE STOREY
(1918- 1991)

A very attractive and pert blonde, June Storey became Gene Autry's female co-star in ten of the singing cowboy's popular Republic western musicals during the period between 1939-40. Among these Autry films were *Blue Montana Skies* (1939), *Rancho Grande* (1940), and *Ride, Tenderfoot, Ride* (194)). A good horse and a loaded six-gun may have been the primary tools of a cowboy hero, however...it was the attentions of a beautiful woman that many times spurred the hero into action. And, often, it was she who rode away with him into the sunset. June was Gene's leading lady during the time he was the top cowboy attraction in the country. Subsequently, she played opposite Ken Curtis before he became internationally famous as "Festus" on the weekly television show, Gunsmoke. Born on April 20, 1918 in Toronto, Canada, Mary June was the youngest of two children born to Lareta and William Storey. "Making westerns," she said, "always seemed very natural to me. I loved the outdoors, and I have only fond memories of the cowboys." She died on December 18, 1991 in Vista, CA.

NELL O'DAY
(1909- 1989)

Nell O'Day was born on September 22, 1909 in Prairie Hill, TX. All of us that love the B-Westerns lost another one of our favorite western Heroines and leading ladies when Nell O'Day passed away quietly on January 3, 1989 in Los Angeles. At her request, no memorial services were held. Nell once said, "I shall always think of the western films I made with great affection. There were wonderful people who worked with me in those films. I think we all felt a strong sense of history as we acted in our western films, knowing that we were making a contribution to the recreation of the history of another time." When Universal was searching for an actress to appear with its star Johnny Mack Brown in a series of western oaters, petite Nell O'Day won out over a dozen others who had tested for the role. Since Nell was an expert equestrian, she had no trouble adapting to her roles, and very often she and Brown did their own stunts. These westerns were very popular and a second series followed as a result.

P-3-60

PEGGY STEWART
(1923-)

Peggy Stewart (born June 5, 1923 in Palm Beach, FL) was the first love of millions of moviegoers in the years 1944 through 1952. Even after these dates, she still is very popular with old westerns. Peggy, a very beautiful brunette, was the heroine in more than sixty of the B-Western that starred the likes of Gene Autry, Sunset Carson, Allan "Rocky" Lane, Wild Bill Elliott, Lash LaRue and Jim Bannon. She also backed up Charles Starrett as his leading lady. Peggy was also well known for her appearances in the early TV series *The Cisco Kid* with Duncan Renaldo. Later, you could have spotted her in television shows like *Quincy*, *Lou Grant*, and some specials. Peggy was at her best in westerns more than the other type of movies. Her acting style allowed her to adapt to those roles with ease. Peggy was an excellent rider and she wore her western outfits as if she was born to them.

ANNE JEFFREYS
(1923-   )

Anne Jeffreys' given name was Anne Jeffreys Carmichael when she was born on January 26, 1923 in Goldsboro, NC. Her first film was a Buster Crabbe western. She didn't enjoy the roles given to her by Republic Studio — chorus girls or gangster's girls, and asked to play a "nice-girl role" for a change. She got the break she wanted when she appeared in her first westerns — an eight picture series with Wild Bill Elliott: *Trail Street*, *Return of the Badmen* and Zane Grey's *Nevada* opposite Robert Mitchum. Of her westerns, Nevada was the most fun to make; it was Mitchum's first starring role. He also had two great sidekicks to support him — Guinn "Big Boy" Williams and Tim Holt's favorite sidekick, Richard Martin. *Nevada* was shot on location in a beautiful spot near Mt. Whitney, and the cast and crew stayed in a small town called Lone Pine, California. (It's not that small now!) Anne did dozens of stage shows including, *The King and I*, *Camelot*, and *The Sound of Music*. At the time of this writing she appears in a running part as Amanda Barrington on the daytime soap *General Hospital*. She remains a beautiful and talented lady.

CHAPTER 12

THE COWBOY AND HIS HORSE

A SAMPLING OF 101

1.	Hopalong Cassidy	Topper
1B.	Mrs. Hoppy	Turnabout
2.	Roy Rogers	Trigger
3.	Gene Autry	Champion
4.	Allen "Rocky" Lane	Black Jack
5.	Wild Bill Elliott	Thunder
6.	The Lone Ranger	Silver
7.	Rex Allen	Koko
8.	Sunset Carson	Cactus
9.	Tom Mix	Tony
10.	Buck Jones	Silver

11.	Ken Maynard	Tarzan
12.	Tex Ritter	White Flash
13.	Monte Hale	Pardner
14.	Jimmy Wakely	Sonny
15.	Andy Clyde	Johnny
16.	Bob Baker	Apache
17.	Tonto	Scout
18.	Don "Red" Barry	Cyclone
19.	Tom Kenne	Rusty
20.	Jack Perrin	Starlight
21.	Fred Thomson	Silver King
22.	William S. Hart	Fritz
23.	Jack Luden	Pal
24.	Guinn "Big Boy" Williams	Rex
25.	Dorothy Page	Snowy
26.	Fred Scott	White King
27.	Bill Cody	Chico
28.	Herbert Jeffery	Stardusk
29.	The Cisco Kid	Diablo
30.	Johnny Mack Brown	Rebel
31.	Poncho	Loco
32.	Little Beaver	Papoose
34.	Bob Steele	Zane
35.	Slim Pickens	Dear John
36.	George O'Brien	Mike

37.	Nell O'Day	Shorty
38.	Peggy Stewart	Smoky
39.	Gail Davis	Target
40.	Charles Starrett	Raider
41.	Bob Livingston	Shamrock
42.	Buster Crabbe	Falcon
43.	Eddie Dean	Flash
44.	Tim Holt	Lighting
45.	Lash LaRue	Black Diamond
46.	Tim McCoy	Midnight
47.	Whip Wilson	Silver Bullet
48.	Smiley Burnette	Ringeye
49.	Tom Tyler	Ace
50.	Bob Foran	Smoke
51.	Andy Devine	Joker
52.	Guy Madison	Buckshot
53.	Jock Mahoney	Rawhide
54.	Buddy Roosevelt	Partner
55.	Jack Randall	Rusty
56.	Bill Boyd	Texas
57.	Reb Russell	Rebel
58.	Jack Holt	Robin Hood
59.	Hoot Gibson	Goldie
60.	Buffalo Bill	Isham
61.	Art Accord	Raven

62.	Bob Allen	Pal
63.	Slim Andrews	Josephine
64.	Tom Baker	Baron
65.	Smith Ballew	Sheik
66.	Rod Cameron	Knight
67.	Pete Morrison	Lightning
68.	Zorro	Tornado
69.	Don Coleman	Ghost
70.	Rex Bell	Silver Pride
71.	Ken Curtis	Thundercloud
72.	Raymond Hatton	Tex
73.	George "Gabby" Hayes	Eddie
74.	Dennis Moore	Cloudy
75.	Rex Lease	Sunday
76.	Wally Wales	Silver King
77.	Jack Hoxie	Bunk
78.	Al Hoxie	Pardner
79.	Russell Hayden	Fritz
80.	William Desmond	Shamrock
81.	Tommy Cook	Cricket
82.	Lane Chandler	Raven
83.	Leo Carillo	Sui Sun
84.	Harry Carey	Sunny
85.	John Carroll	Loco
86.	Buffalo Bill, Jr.	Chilli

87.	Buzz Barton	White Cloud
88.	Jim Bannon	Thunder
89.	Ben Johnson	Blackie
90.	Richard "Chito" Martin	Taco
91.	Kermit Maynard	Rocky
92.	Monte Montana	Rex
93.	Will Rogers	Soap Suds
94.	James Stewart	Pie
95.	Roy Stewart	Ranger
96.	Randy Scott	Star Dust
97.	Dale Evans	Buttermilk
98.	John Wayne	Duke
99.	James Arness	Old Buck
100.	Dale Robertson	Jubilee

BURY ME NOT
ON THE LONE PRAIRIE

Oh bury me not on the lone prairie
These words came low and mournfully
From the pallid lips of a youth who lay
On his dying bed at the close of day.

He has wasted an pined 'til o'er his brow
Heath's shades were slowly gathering now.
He thought of home and love ones nigh,
And the cowboys gathered to see him die.

Oh bury me not on the lone prairie,
Where the coyotes howl and the wind blows free.
In a narrow grave just six by three
Oh bury me not on the lone prairie.

It matters not, I've oft been told,
Where the body lies when the heart grows cold.
Yet grant, oh grant, this wish to me,
Oh bury me not on the lone prairie.

THE COWBOY AND HIS HORSE

I've always wished to be laid when I died
In a little churchyard on a green hillside.
By my father's grave there let me be,
Oh bury me not on the lone prairie.

I wish to lie where a mother's prayer
And a sister's tear will mingle there.
Where friends can come and weep o'er me.
Oh bury me not on the lone prairie.

For there's another whose tears will shed
For the one who lies in a prairie bed.
It breaks my heart to think of her now,
She has curled these locks; she has kissed this brow.

Oh bury me not...." And his voice failed there.
But they took no heed to his dying prayer.
In a narrow grave, just six by three,
They buried him there on the lone prairie.

And the cowboys now as they roam the plain
For they marked the spot where his bones were lain,
Fling a handful of roses o'er his grave
With a prayer to God, his soul to save.